SAPPHIRE SPHERE: PORTAL TO ETERNITY

Part I
LEARNING TO CONNECT

Part II
STAYING CONNECTED

SAPPHIRE SPHERE: PORTAL TO ETERNITY

You Can Open Doorways Into The Invisible Realms
Be Careful How You Open

Expanded version of

You Can Actually Be With God: How to Receive the Holy Spirit; Talk to God and Have Him Answer (c. 1976, and 2005, edited and revised, 2011)

and

"The Inner Room" from *Six Nights Till Morning: The Real Star Wars* (c. 1983, 1984, pp. 260-289, edited and revised, 2011)

By
Norbert H. Kox

"LOVE"

אהב
AHB
Apocalypse House Books
New Franken, WI

SAPPHIRE SPHERE: PORTAL TO ETERNITY
You Can Open Doorways Into The Invisible Realms
Be Careful How You Open

Copyright 2014 by Norbert H, Kox, All rights reserved.

Expanded version of *You Can Actually Be With God: How to Receive the Holy Spirit; Talk to God and Have Him Answer* (c. 1976, and 2005, edited and revised, 2011) and "The Inner Room" from *Six Nights Till Morning: The Real Star Wars* (c. 1983, 1984, pp. 260-289, edited and revised, 2011).

No part of this book may be used or reproduced in any manner whatsoever without written permission of the publisher, except in the case of brief quotations in articles and reviews. For information, write: Apocalypse House, P.O. Box 109, New Franken, WI 54229.

ISBN: 978-1-936810-01-7

Library of Congress Control Number: 2014917268

Please visit our website: **www.apocalypsehouse.com**
For information regarding author interviews, please contact:
nhkox@yahoo.com

Cover design and all artwork by Norbert H. Kox
Cover: Based on Arc of the Ark, 2007, Acrylic on canvas.

Apocalypse House
New Franken, WI

ACKNOWLEDGEMENTS

My first thanks are to God, who commissioned this work and guided my research. Thanks to all the writers and researchers, living and dead, whose invaluable work has made possible the compilation of *Sapphire Sphere: Portal to Eternity*. Thanks to Nancy Kolosso, who did the original typing of *Six Nights Till Morning: The Real Star Wars*, the 900-page manuscript which first included "The Inner Room" (c. 1983) and to my proofreaders George E. Meyer and Jeremy J. Kox. May God send his blessings on all that were involved in this project and upon everyone that reads these pages.

DEDICATION

This book is dedicated to the glory and honor of Yesu Christ, and to my dearly departed brother in Christ, Keith W. Kraus (Bud), who was the proofreader of *Six Nights Till Morning: The Real Star Wars*, which included "The Inner Room" and "Who Changed God's Name."

Bud was a true brother. Simultaneously, he and I came into the truths of the Sabbath and the Name. We were so struck by the importance that on March 6, 1982, in 20-degree weather, we shoveled two feet of snow off a creek in Northern Wisconsin and chopped a hole through 12 inches of solid ice, to re-baptize each other by immersion in the name of Yesu Christ. It was the greatest day in our lives.

In the more than thirty years to follow, there have been great obstacles, challenges and tribulations with new struggles arising every day. I thank God for allowing this writing to be completed for his glory and yours.

God bless all my brothers and sisters, in Bimini and around the world, along with everyone who puts his hands on this book and sets his heart to contemplate these writings. You are already on the path; may we persevere till the end.

TABLE OF CONTENTS

VII ACKNOWLEDGEMENTS & DEDICATION
XI ABOUT THE AUTHOR
XII INTRODUCTION
XIV THE CALLING

Part I: LEARNING TO CONNECT

19 SAPPHIRE SPHERE
20 DIVINE SYSTEM OF SPONTANEOUS REGENERATION
23 GOD IS IN YOU
23 GOOD NEWS
24 SECRET PLACE
24 SPIRITUAL BURGLARY
26 INNER ROOM CHAMBER
27 NO RELIGION TOO
30 THE SOURCE
31 ALL IN SYMMETRY
33 HEAVENLY VIBRATIONS
37 SOLID ENERGY
38 COLLIDING REALMS
40 PORTAL OF HEAVEN
42 ENERGIZE THE PORTAL – RIVER OF LIGHT
45 THE BLUE STAR (SAPPHIRE SPHERE)
47 STUMBLING IN THE LIGHT
48 THE VISITATION
52 INSIGHTS
55 CHOOSING A MANTRA
58 SEEING THE FATHER
59 HEAVENLY VOWEL NAME
60 FLOW OF THE BREATH
61 PRAYER BREATHING
61 MAKE ROOM FOR GOD
63 GOD WITHIN
65 A WORD ABOUT TM
65 SPELLING OUT BRAINWAVES
68 DARK NIGHT OF THE SOUL
70 FEELING THE PRESENCE OF GOD
72 ONCE YOU REACH GOD DO NOT SLACK OFF

Part II: STAYING CONNECTED

75 NAME ABOVE EVERY NAME
75 THE NAME OF SALVATION
76 THE INDESTRUCTiBLE NAME
79 HIS EXISTENCE AND GIFT
79 CLOUD OF UNKNOWING
80 BREAKTHROUGH
81 INTO THE INNER ROOM
82 CLEANING HOUSE
82 SPIRIT BAPTISM
85 CRITICAL ANSWERS
86 CHURCH OF THE SPIRIT
88 TAKING ON THE BRIDEGROOM'S NAME
89 SPIRIT AND THE WORD
90 CLEANSE THE TEMPLE
90 BE A SAINT NOT A SINNER
91 THE CODE OF THE HEART CAN BE CHANGED

94 BACK-WORD: THE END FROM THE BIGINNING
94 EPILOGUE: SEVENTY-FOUR WITNESSES
95 LAST WORD: FEELING UNWORTHY
97-99 NOTES: Record Your Own Thoughts Here

LIST OF IMAGES

Artworks by Norbert H. Kox

XIII **Blood Offering: Yesu Christ the Sacrificial Lamb**
   1976-1988, acrylic and oil on canvas, 96" x 48"
Exhibitions:
   1988, Lawton Gallery, University of Wisconsin-Green Bay
   1989, Wisconsin Gallery of Art, Milwaukee Art Museum
   1990, *Religious Visionaries*, John Michael Kohler Arts Center, Sheboygan, WI
   1991, *47th Art Annual*, Neville Museum, Green Bay, WI
   1992, Green Bay Blue Art Gallery, Green Bay, WI
   1993, People's Choice Art Gallery, De Pere, Wisconsin
   1996, Bradley Gallery of Art, Lakeland College, Sheboygan, WI
   1996, *Augeries of the Next Apocalypse*, Dean Jensen Gallery, Milwaukee, WI
   1998, *Apocalypse of a Ravaged Society*, Wisconsin Academy Gallery, Madison, WI
   1999, *To Hell and Back*, Neville Museum, Green Bay, WI
   2000, *Wisconsin Classic*, Milwaukee Institute of Art and Design
   2008, *Miracles of the Spirit*, Cultural Arts Center, Whitewater, WI

21 **Divine System of Spontaneous Regeneration**
   2005-2006, acrylic on canvas, 60" x 108"
Exhibitions:
   2006, *Divine System of Spontaneous Regeneration*, Ministry of Education, Bimini, Bahamas
   2011-2012, *Divine*, Webb Gallery, Waxahatchie, Texas
   2014, *The Visionary Experience: Saint Francis to Finster*, American Visionary Art Museum

29 **Tree of Life**
   2006-2007, acrylic on canvas, 48" x 36"
Exhibitions:
   2007, *Crossing the Strait*, Ministry of Education, Bimini, Bahamas
   2008, *Sacred Pastures*, Horse Hospital, London, England
   2008, *Eloquent Obsessions*, Orleans House, Richmond, England

34 **Brain Heart: The Heavenly Portal**
   2010-2011, acrylic on canvas, 63" x 41"
Exhibitions:
   2011, *Holy Spirit Manifesting*, Ministry of Education, Bimini, Bahamas
   2011, *Adventures, Reflections and Ambushes*, Le Manoir de la Ville, Martigny, Switzerland
   2012, *High Time*, Galerie TOXIC, Luxembourg, Luxembourg
   2012, *HEY! Modern Art & Pop Culture / Part II*, The Museum Halle Saint Pierre, Paris, France

ABOUT THE AUTHOR

Norbert H. Kox was born in Green Bay, Wisconsin on August 6, 1945, the same day the atomic bomb was dropped on Hiroshima. By age seventeen, Kox was an alcoholic. He quit high school in 1962 and joined the army, where in his spare time he taught himself to paint in the Service Club art center at Warner Kaserne, Munich, Germany. This included studying how-to manuals. After his stint in the service, he continued to drink heavily while working on custom cars and motorcycles for a living. Kox became a member of the Waterloo Outlaws biker gang, but "hit bottom" by his thirtieth birthday after a bad drug trip. He swore off alcohol and drugs, gave away most of his possessions and retreated to the wilderness. For the next ten years he meditated and lived by himself in the woods near Suring, Wisconsin. Here he built a personal chapel and a "Gospel Road" with scripture-based messages leading through the forest to a gruesome life-sized sculpture of the crucifixion. Around 1980 he joined a conservative Pentecostal Christian group and continued his Bible studies. In 1985, he returned to Green Bay to pursue an education at the University of Wisconsin, where he studied geology, religion and writing, but finished in art, after which he took up painting full-time as his way of life. At age sixty-eight, 2013 marked his 50th year as an artist. (American Visionary Art Museum)

According to his website, Kox's artwork and writings "...denounce idolatry and hypocrisy as sins of organized religion," and his "APOCALYPTIC VISUAL PARABLES are a prophetic revelation, or apocalypse of the end times." Kox believes that his works "...reveal that much of modern Christianity has been duped by the Adversary and has actually become the religion of the Antichrist. The world stands in judgment, with change on one side of the balance, and destruction on the other." (*ibid.*)

INTRODUCTION

The first version of this treatise was published in 1976, after experiencing a miraculous deliverance from alcohol addiction, drugs and a life of total despair. A true spiritual regeneration transpired and I was eager and enthusiastic to share this newfound source of freedom and joy with the world. Being anxious to help others, I sprang forth without sufficient knowledge. I was not even sure of what had happened to me, and was already trying to tell others about it.

My original manuscript contained some Marian references, as might be expected since I had been raised in Catholicism. Most of these references and quotations have been removed from this revision, being unscriptural. More than 35 years of Biblical study and research have allowed me to see through the dark areas of Catholicism and traditional Christianity, and have enlightened me to many hidden truths. Scripture is the measuring line by which to test the spirits to see if they are of God (1 John 4: 1).

Even our Bibles must be tested with Scripture. Our vernacular translations fall short, and must be tested against the oldest existing Hebrew and Greek manuscripts to ascertain the proper rendition. Today, practically anyone can acquire the necessary tools from a Christian bookstore, or Amazon.com, to be able to make these critical comparisons. A *Strong's Exhaustive Concordance* should be first on the list. Next, obtain Greek and Hebrew interlinear Bibles. They have the original languages with English translations beneath each word. This in itself will be helpful, but to go even deeper, additional Hebrew and Greek dictionaries will be useful. This will take most students as deep as they would like. The next step would be Hebrew and Greek grammar books. Deep study does not appeal to everybody, and most will go no deeper than their English version of the Bible. This is fine. Just be aware that all English Bibles are strewn with inaccuracies.

XIII

XIV

Shortly after my spiritual genesis and the writing of *You Can Actually Be With God: How to Receive the Holy Spirit; Talk to God and Have Him Answer* (1976) God allowed me a vision of the crucifixion of Christ in all its horrifying detail. It was more than a vision. It seemed to be a portal experience. It was as if I were transported in time and space to Golgotha, the place of the skull, and was actually there at Christ's crucifixion. At that very instant I was commissioned by means of a thought injection from God, to paint the scene so that others could see the brutality of what really happened. Most of the painting was completed within one year (additional details were added in 1988). The title is, *Blood Offering: Yesu Christ the Sacrificial Lamb* (previous page; acrylic and oil on canvas, 96" x 48").

THE CALLING

God led me into the wilderness on approximately a ten year hermitage, to be nurtured and taught by his Holy Spirit while spending untold hours in meditation, prayer and intense Biblical research. Then he brought me back into society in 1986, to begin to share what he had revealed to me.

I returned to the University of Wisconsin in Green Bay, where I started out in science but turned later to writing and received a degree in journalism. Continuing my education, I transferred to the Art department where I felt inspired to paint Apocalyptic Visual Parables. These paintings were an outgrowth of my first masterpiece (*Blood Offering: Yesu Christ the Sacrificial Lamb*) with the intent of exposing falsehoods and revealing truths.

Many of my paintings have negative and evil imagery in them, but it is always used as a warning. It points out evil and harmful things that might be stumbling blocks and pitfalls for people, and gives warning against them so as to alert people that something is wrong and they must be careful to avoid these things. The dark imagery is not meant to draw people to darkness but rather to sound an alarm against it. Like a skull and cross bones on a poison bottle, it warns you not to take this internally; and may save your life. The negative imagery of the skull and cross bones has become positive because it was used as a warning against the possibility of being poisoned. That is also how my paintings work. Most of my paintings have Scripture verses in them or at least passage references so that interested persons can start an investigation into the truth. The intention of all my artwork is to stimulate the viewer into a deeper search for truth. So it is not utterly important that the viewer agrees with me but rather that he or she is stirred enough to start an investigation of their own.

During my wilderness hermitage I had written a 900-page book with the same intent. *Six Nights Till Morning: The Real Star Wars* was self-published in 1983 and revised in 1984. Only a few copies existed. It is in the process of additional revisions now, to be re-published in segments. The book you are holding, *Sapphire Sphere: Portal To Eternity*, was originally published in pamphlet form by the title, *You Can Actually Be With God: How to Receive the Holy Spirit; Talk to God and Have Him Answer*, and also in "The Inner Room" chapter in *Six Nights Till Morning: The Real Star Wars*. It is an introductory volume to the forthcoming series.

This version, *Sapphire Sphere: Portal to Eternity* has been written and compiled with the intention of helping others to connect with the presence of our Creator, through proven methods of prayer and meditation, thus unlocking a door that has been closed for too long. This connection will give new hope and new life. It will release you from all fear of death and the unknown.

This book may not be for everyone, but it was written with everyone in mind. There are many references to Christ, so if you are not a believer this may cause some hesitation. Do not let this stop you from reading. Even if you are an Atheist you may have some lingering questions hidden in the back of your mind. So just read and see what answers may appear, or what new questions may develop. Whatever walk of life you are in whatever religion or non-religion there is something in the Sapphire Sphere for you.

SAPPHIRE SPHERE: PORTAL TO ETERNITY

Part I

LEARNING TO CONNECT

SAPPHIRE SPHERE

The sapphire sphere is a spiritual reference that relates to one of the highest forms of divine communication. Ancient mystics called it the Tree of Life and Chariot of God, believing it to be a portal entrance.

Genesis 2:9, says the tree of life (in the plural, lives) is in the middle of the garden and the tree of knowledge of good and evil (good and bad knowledge). How can both simultaneously occupy the same space in the center of the garden unless they are one and the same tree? In some of the apocryphal writings the tree of lives is said to contain all the information of the lives of everyone from the beginning to the end, past, present and future. It contains the knowledge of every good and bad act, every good and bad thought throughout all of time.

The *tree* (עץ) of life, *plan* (עץ) of life, was pictured by our ancestors with ten connected spheres and an eleventh invisible sphere called *daath*, "knowledge." The Hebrew word for spheres is *sephirot*. The singular spelling of sphere is, ספירה (right to left). In fact, phonetically, ספיר can be pronounced "sphere." ספיר is also the spelling in Hebrew for sapphire. So basically sapphire and sphere are the same word. Each of the eleven sapphire spheres is a type of spiritual portal with the center *tiferet* being the connecting point between heaven and earth. *Tiferet* is an eight-spoked wheel indicating that it is the point where flesh becomes spirit and vice versa. It is also guarded by the archangel Auriel (Hebrew, "Lights of God"). Auriel is the guardian of the passage between heaven and earth.

DIVINE SYSTEM OF SPONTANEOUS REGENERATION

In the winter of 2005-2006, came the inspiration to paint the symbolic image of God transmuted into the tree/plan of life and the blueprint of man. This is the same pattern of energy that is imprinted upon the beds we each sleep in. We each have our own pattern of positive or negative energy. The heavenly lines of energy from God that connect to this pattern actually recharge us as we sleep. It is the divine system of spontaneous regeneration. The energy of the universe will respond to our attitude and treat us accordingly. If we have imprinted negativity into our pattern we will have problem areas at the points where the bad energy is. This can even cause health problems for us, both physically and mentally. We can ask God to change negative or non-beneficial energy to beneficial and through prayer and attitude it will be done. This has nothing to do with spiritual salvation. It is all part of the laws of the universe laid out by the Creator to benefit all of mankind, "...he maketh his sun to rise on the evil and on the good, and sendeth rain on the just and on the unjust" (Matthew 5:45).

A symbol of quintessence, or the fifth element, is present in the tree of life. Nine is the number of divine manifestation. The energy lines between the nine primary spheres in the pattern form two stacked tiers of double X's: two side-by-side X's are standing on top of two more. The four X's in that configuration actually create a fifth X at the center of a diamond shape that is made up of four smaller diamonds. The four X's and four diamonds represent the four elements, earth, fire, water, air, while the fifth X and the fifth diamond represent the fifth element, ether.

The four elements represent the physical world we live in, and the fifth element, the quintessence, is the ether, representing the spiritual realm of light and energy. The fifth element symbol is centered on the *sephirot* or sphere named Tiferet, which is at the exact middle of the tree and connects all the other spheres. It also represents a portal between the heavenly and earthly domains. *Tiferet*, תפארת, means adornment, beauty and glory. It is the sixth sphere and corresponds to the Hebrew letter *waw* (or, *vav*) which is another portal symbol linking heaven and earth.

The world we now see was first created of pure energy. According to ancient writings Adam and Eve were made of energy; they were beings of light. After the fall God made them coats of *skins* (Genesis 3:21). In the Hebrew text it is written in the singular, "skin." It is probably not referring to coats sewn together of animal skins, since skin is singular. It may be a reference to beings of light receiving actual skin. Yahweh evidently slowed down their frequencies so that they manifested as flesh and blood physical beings. Like Einstein once said, "What we have called matter is energy, whose vibration has been so lowered as to be perceptible to the senses."

After Adam and Eve had disobeyed God and realized what they had done, they were frightened, and the Bible says, "Adam and his wife hid themselves from the presence of Yahweh God amongst the trees of the garden" (Genesis 3:8). In the Hebrew text we immediately see that it does not say "trees." It is singular "tree" (עץ). They hid "in the middle of the tree of the garden" (בתוך עץ הגן). When we examine the tree of life plan, the *Tiferet* is directly "in the middle of the tree." The man and woman went into the *Tiferet*.

The beams of light from the entire tree all converge into the *Tiferet* possibly making it the brightest spot, a natural place for beings of light to attempt to hide. They unwittingly did exactly what God had planned for them. By going into the portal they were moved by God from the ethereal kingdom of spirit, light and energy into the physical realm of darkness and matter, where they were *coated with skin*. Essentially they had cut themselves off from God and the light, slowing their frequencies and becoming physical beings. (*A Speck of Atlantis: Bimini, The Top Of God's Mountain*, pp.56-57)

GOD IS IN YOU

Believe it or not: God is in you! But he does not force you to acknowledge him. He has given you free will.

You can deny God, but then do not expect God to acknowledge you. He has created you to share this life with him, living in the same body, enjoying life together. But the choice to share is yours. When you make the choice to acknowledge God he will acknowledge you.

God does not just take over your life; you need to decide how much of your life you are willing to give to God. The more you give to God, the more he gives to you. When you give everything so does he. It is a very simple principle: You give nothing, you get nothing.

GOOD NEWS

God has not abandoned you. Most people believe that God is not in a sinful person. You may feel that you have done too much or gone too far, but that is the enemy bringing despair. Regardless of how sinful or evil you may be, God is in you. It is just that you have not made the connection. You must open the door; God does not force it to open.

God is in everyone. That means there is hope for everyone, the hope of glory. God is not spying on us from outer space with a pen and ink writing down our actions in a book of judgment. He is inside of every one of us experiencing our lives. He is witnessing first hand everything we do or say or think. Yes God knows even our thoughts because he is in every cell in our body, mind, and heart. God is omnipresent and is the pure energy of which all things visible and invisible exist. Nothing exists outside of God or without God.

When you open the door and realize the presence of God within you a whole new life begins. Condemnation leaves when the light shines. A change takes place. The Biblical analogy is that the old man (person) dies and a new person emerges, to live in a newness of life. When you change and allow the mind of Christ to direct your path you become a saint.

As sinners we were condemned to death, but as saints we are perfected in Christ to inherit righteousness and glory in the eternal kingdom of God.

SECRET PLACE

> There is a secret place, an inner room, where one can find rest and refreshing, although it is seldom discovered. Man is in such a constant search for rest that he often wears himself out in his rigorous pursuit of escape. (The Inner Room, p.260).

SPIRITUAL BURGLARY

The natural man is living on the surface. He never really discovers how to enter the inner room of calm and peace. "Within the psyche of man are secret rooms, vast chambers full of treasures with windows looking out on eternity and infinity." (*The Master Game,* p.30). To enter into the inner being, through prayer, takes practice and discipline. "The Mystic Way is, by all accounts, hard and long. How much easier it is to break open the locked doors of the secret chambers in the psyche by chemical means?" But this drugging constitutes a kind of "spiritual burglary, a criminal activity on the spiritual level" (*ibid.* p.42), which bears its own hazards and penalties.

Unaware of how to get relief through prayer many have diverted to artificial means of escape. The use of alcohol and drugs are merely attempts to alter the state of consciousness and bring about a feeling of peace or bliss.

Pill pushing doctors become gods to their patients. They are the priests and medicine men, handing out communion of mind-altering substances. They are often guilty of breaking down potentially healthy people by the administering of unnecessary drugs. Sometimes the drugs even make the initial problem worse. Robert S. Mendelsohn, M.D. has stated:

> You should be aware of all the drugs for which the side effects are the same as the indications. This isn't as rare as you might think. For example, if you read the list of indications for Valium, and then read the list of side effects, you'll find that the lists are more or less interchangeable! Under the indications you'll find: anxiety, fatigue, depression, acute agitation tremors, hallucinosis and skeletal muscle spasms. And under the side effects: anxiety, fatigue, depression, acute hyperexcited states, tremors, hallucinations, increased muscle spasticity! I admit I don't know how to use a drug like this: what am I supposed to do if I prescribe it and the symptoms continue? Stop the drug or double the dose? (*Confessions of a Medical Heretic*, p.82).

Many people in search of inner peace will go to a doctor for drugs. They have been taught that this is the way and that pills are the answer to everything. If they do receive any relief, it is only temporary and soon the dosage has to be increased to counteract the side effects. When the drug is no longer effective, the doctor prescribes a stronger one. And so on. When his list of drugs runs out and the patient is worse off than ever, he will recommend a mental facility.

Suffering people who cannot get a legal fix from their doctors often turn to the streets to get their medication from a pusher. Any number of complications may arise and sometimes the users end up dead.

The drugging of the nations continues as man fails to look to the true source of inner peace. While adhering to the life destroying prescriptions of modern medicine, alcohol, and illegal street drugs, he ignores the only prescription of any value, that of prayer and fasting. It is easier to pop a pill, or smoke, or snort, or drink than to put forth the necessary effort in prayer.

INNER ROOM CHAMBER

People's minds are troubled because they cannot gain access to the inner room. Even the majority of very religious people are living in the outer court, when they could be dwelling in the Holy of Holies. They know not how to enter the temple of God or the secret place of the most High. "The Divine Reality is hidden in darkness behind a curtain of religious belief and practice that seems a dreary and chilling system of abstract propositions, formulas empty and merely verbal, meaningless distinctions, minutiae of a formalist ritual, mechanical or perfunctory prayers, a public worship that is no more than a social convention." (*A Philosophy of Form*, p.416).

Yesu said, "when thou prayest, enter into thy *inner chambers*, and when thou hast shut thy door, pray to thy Father which is in secret" (Matthew 6: 6). God does not dwell in temples made by man. You are his temple. God is omnipresent and dwells in everyone, even if they have not received the baptism of the Holy Spirit. If one can achieve access to the inner room and the presence of God, he can attain the perfect high. Drugs and alcohol suddenly become unnecessary, even undesirable; in fact, the whole physical world loses its seductiveness.

The highest form of prayer is contemplation/meditation. It is in contemplation that man is visited by God and there is a uniting of the

Divine Nature (Creator) with the created. God is always there, we just need to establish communication.

NO RELIGION TOO

Mankind has always wondered about its creator and has established religious practices in an attempt to please God. Some religions were formulated to extend control over the populace. The world has been filled with religions: 10,000 of which Christianity is one. The Christian religion is split into 33,000 denominations (*World Christian Encyclopedia*, vol.1, p.16). So the one religion that is supposed to be united has more divisions than all the religions in the world.

This Babylon of religious confusion has left many people in a state of bewilderment as to which way is the true path. Others have sedated themselves with the doctrines of man, so they find comfort in the "safety" of their indoctrinations. Some just feel it does not matter which direction a person takes, and others think it is all a bunch of foolishness. But men have always been filled with wonderment and have tried in some way to communicate with our creator.

Today we are all lost in the fog of this material world. "Things" block our vision. We *know* too much. All knowledge, especially religious knowledge, will hinder the perfect communion of oneness with God. The more we know, see and have, the further we get from the path of true enlightenment. We have to unlearn in order to unburden and unshackle our inner self, which is able to guide us on the pathway of the eternal.

An anonymous fourteenth century mystic wrote a treatise which instructed methods of clearing the mind of all baggage, good and evil, to come into the place of visitation where God communes with his creation. We have to at least temporarily become unattached to all that is of this world, even our Godly and holy thoughts. We must be free of all earthly and human thoughts to enter the inner sanctum and the presence of God. Anything at all that we "know" will simply be in the way and must be abandoned. "If you are to experience him or to see him at all, insofar as it is possible here, it must always be in this cloud and in this darkness." (*The Cloud of Unknowing*).

No amount of reasoning, knowledge, wisdom, petitioning or pleading can open the secret doorway to the Eternal. It is only with humbleness, obedience and surrender that the door can be opened and the veil penetrated. And it is all in simplicity. No formula, no ritual, no initiation can get you in. You are the temple. God is inside of you. You are not going to meet him outside or in an earthly edifice. You must go within, and the only way in is through the void, the frightening silence and darkness between you and the inner self. You have to first get past all the commotion hiding in the corners of your mind, and go so deeply into your own inner being, beyond all, until you reach the depth were nothing else can possibly exist, and you will be at the point of the beginning and the ending of all things, *where there is no beginning or end*, eternity. At this point time and space are no longer relevant. There is no difference between the infinitely small and infinitely large. It is the source of the Eternal, the seed and essence of all things. It is here, beyond the veil in the holy of holies, where God engages you without words, in an embrace of pure unselfish agape love and enlightenment.

The way is simple. It is always with you. The ancient Chinese called it Tao (dow), the Way or the Path. In Chinese writing the character for Tao is a composite of two characters, which literally means "proceeding from the head." Tao is both the source and the way, the essence of all things. It is the plan of God that directs all things in the universe. It is more than God's plan. It is God himself. It is everything. When we live the plan, the way, the Tao, we are in unity with our Creator.

This is not to advocate or promote Taoism as such, but simply uses the word Tao because of its meaning and significance. Although, upon study of several different translations of the *Tao Teh Ching* writings, they were found to compliment rather than contradict the Bible.

Tree Of Life
2006-2007, Acrylic on Canvas, 48" x 36"

Exhibitions: Bimini, Bahamas, 2007, Ministry of Education; London, England: *Sacred Pastures*, 2008, Horse Hospital Gallery; Richmond, England: *Eloquent Obsessions*, 2008, Orleans House.

THE SOURCE

"There exists a Being undifferentiated and complete, born before heaven and earth. Tranquil, boundless, abiding alone and changing not, encircling everything without exhaustion. Fathomless, it seems to be the Source of all things. I do not know its name, but characterize it as the Tao. Arbitrarily forcing a name upon it, I call it Great." (*Tao Teh Ching*, ch.25, from, *Christ The Eternal Tao*, p.6).

"In the beginning was the Tao, and the Tao was with God, and the Tao was God....And the Tao became flesh, and dwelt among us..." (John 1:1, 14; *translated from a Canton edition of the NT, published in China in 1911 by the American Bible Society*; cited here from, *Christ The Eternal Tao*, p.8).

Christ said, "I am the way, the truth, and the life, no man comes unto the father but by me." In Chinese terms, he said, "I am the Tao, the truth, and the Chi [life-force]."

Yahweh promised to put his plan, his way, his Tao within us. He is inside of us to lead and guide our path.

"For this is the covenant that I will make with the house of Israel after those days, saith Yahweh; I will put my laws into their mind, and write them in their hearts: and I will be to them a God, and they shall be to me a people: And they shall not teach every man his neighbor, and every man his brother, saying, Know Yahweh: for all shall know me, from the least to the greatest." (Hebrews 8:10-11)

"For when the Gentiles, which have not the law, do by nature the things contained in the law, these, having not the law, are a law unto themselves: Which shew the work of the law written in their hearts, their conscience also bearing witness, and their thoughts [consciences] the mean while accusing or else excusing one another." (Romans 2:14-15)

"Howbeit when he, the Spirit of truth, is come, he will guide you into all truth: for he shall not speak of himself; but whatsoever he shall hear, that shall he speak: and he will shew you things to come." (John 16:13).

"Even the Spirit of truth; whom the world cannot receive, because it seeth him not, neither knoweth him: but ye know him; for he dwelleth with you, and shall be in you. I will not leave you comfortless: I will come to you. Yet a little while, and the world seeth me no more; but ye see me: because I live, ye shall live also. At that day ye shall know that I am in my Father, and ye in me, and I in you." (John 14:17-20)

The inner voice of the Tao is our evidence that God is with us and in us, and we in him. Always be very cautious and careful to recognize the leading, whether it is truly of God. If something violates another's rights you must resist. You can not always go with the flow. There is a deceptive voice of self-will that contradicts the Tao. Ego distorts the vision. There is also a subtle voice of the enemy that contradicts, and counterfeits, the Spirit of Tao. Beware.

ALL IN SYMMETRY

Everything is done symmetrically. All through Scripture God works in pairs, twins, juxtapositions. Things are done in symmetry, beginning in Genesis with darkness and light, good and evil, Cain and Abel; then progressing and culminating with Christ and Antichrist, and finally at judgment, eternal death versus eternal life.

To the Chinese, Tao is the symmetry of Yin and Yang, female/male, dark/light, night/day, negative/positive, discharge/charge, death/life, etc. There are always opposites. The spirit realm is a world of life, the kingdom of God. Its opposite is the physical world, a realm of death, Satan's domain. Any adept Bible scholar will tell you this world is under the control of Satan. When Yesu said, "My kingdom is not of this world," it was because Satan is master of the physical realm, the material world of death. Yesu's kingdom of God is light and life.

Why is this earth presently Satan's realm and kingdom? Adam and Eve were given dominion over everything on earth (Genesis 1:28) but relinquished that power to Satan when they submitted themselves to the serpent in Eden. By not exercising their power of control over Satan they actually surrendered to him and gave him superiority over this world, so that he could later say to Yesu Christ, concerning all the kingdoms of this world, "All this power will I give thee, and the glory of them: for that is delivered unto me; and to whomsoever I will I give it. If thou therefore wilt worship me, all shall be thine." (Luke 4:6-7).

"And Yesu answered and said unto him, Get thee behind me, Satan: for it is written, Thou shalt worship Yahweh thy God, and him only shalt thou serve." (Luke 4:8).

Pilate asked Yesu, "Are you the king of the Jews?" He answered, "My kingdom is not of this world." (John 18:36).

There is the kingdom of God (spiritual) and there is the kingdom of Satan (material). They do not mix.

The two kingdoms exist simultaneously in the same space. One is eternal; the other is time-driven. God, as Source, is pure energy perpetually emitting light, in waves of various frequencies that sustain all of existence.

Yesu Christ is the Pyramidion Portal, the Capstone Crown (Keter; the 10th Sphere) the Ehyeh (I Am/I Will Be) the first Begotten which came forth from En Soph (Nothingness) to be the Creator, the Author and Finisher of all things including our salvation.

Entering the spiritual portal, we go through the first Sphere, Malkhut (Kingdom) which allows us to climb the ladder of the tree of life all the way to the Crown/Capstone. The moment we enter Malkhut we are in the Holy Place and in union with the *Shekhinah*,

Divine Presence. Once inside the portal we have full access to all the Sapphire Spheres (in essence, all are one) to freely absorb the benefits and blessings of the Tree of Life.

HEAVENLY VIBRATIONS

> He that dwelleth in the secret place of the most High shall abide under the shadow of the Almighty. (Psalms 91:1).

Can we really access the invisible realms of heaven? Can the spiritual and physical realms exist simultaneously in the same time and space? Normally we cannot see the spirit realm and angels even when they are right in front of us because of their extremely high frequency. In such an environment our natural physical bodies would be instantly disintegrated that is why scripture says we will be changed (1Corinthians 15:50-54). Only in a glorified immortal body like the risen Christ could we survive "heaven" without burning up.

We may enter now spiritually but not bodily, unless we are specially protected by the Almighty, like Enoch was.

The *Brain Heart* painting (Kox, 2010-2011) illustrates how the brain and the heart are tied together in a complex communication system that produces electrical frequencies linked to the spiritual realm.

Lao Tzu, mystic philosopher of ancient China, described a small "gateway to heaven and earth" in the center of the brain behind the eyes.

The pineal gland is at the exact geometrical center of the brain.

French philosopher Rene Descartes suggested that the pineal gland is the "seat of the soul" (1649). Modern scientists have discovered a correlation between pineal gland activation and spiritual meditation. They have also discovered that when subjects enter the meditative state and experience visions and feelings of the presence of God,

Brain Heart: The Heavenly Portal
2010-2011, Acrylic on Canvas, 63" x 41"

Exhibitions: Bimini, Bahamas, 2011, Ministry of Education; Martigny, Switzerland, 2011, Le Manoir de la Ville; Luxembourg, Luxembourg, 2012, Galerie Toxic; Paris, France, 2013, *HEY! Modern Art & Pop Culture / Part II*, The Museum Halle Saint Pierre their brains produce specific and distinct electromagnetic wave patterns from the temporal lobes. This is the area of the *amygdala* (Greek, almond) almond-shaped groups of nuclei located deep within the medial temporal lobes of the brain.

When these same frequencies are artificially introduced into the brain using computerized electromagnets, they sometimes stimulate visions and otherworldly experiences including the presence of God. This is not an indication that God exists only in the brain, but rather that the brain is a communication system between the visible and invisible realms and that specific stimulation whether through meditation or artificial means may open a portal to the spiritual.

Dr. J. Andrew Armour, in 1991, revealed that the heart contains an area of neurons, neurotransmitters and cells exactly like those of the brain that qualify it as a "little brain" in the heart. It can act independently of the cranial brain to "learn, remember, feel and sense." The heart communicates with the brain via nerves in the spinal column.

Many scriptural references speak of the heart thinking and feeling.

The brain in the heart and brain in the head work in unison to create impulses that can open portals to spiritual realms and act as a communication system to the heavenly. Positive thinking, faith and belief are keys that open the veil.

In Genesis chapter 28, Jacob saw angels ascending and descending through the portal of heaven. This was at a place called Luz (almond tree) which is also the Hebrew word for "gland." Jacob called it *Bethel*, the house of God. He experienced the portal again when he wrestled with God at *Peniel* (Gen. 32) which is Hebrew for "the face of God," and is also the Hebrew spelling for pineal.

Peniel is a reference to the pineal gland, or as Descartes called it "the seat of the soul." One of the English pronunciations of pineal is exactly the same as the Hebrew peniel, "the face of God." Jacob's experiences of the presence, or face of God, are an analogy to the pineal gland (*luz-peniel*).

The pineal gland secrets a fluid that is much responsible for dreams and visions. The gland is suspended in a cavern in the middle of the brain, like the Ark of the Covenant in the Holy of Holies, and metaphorically you are the temple of God.

Every individual undergoes some sort of spiritual experience at some point in his or her life, although the majority will be reluctant to talk about it. Our minds are like radio and television receivers to the psychic realm. Some are more sensitive and finely tuned than others. Everyone receives mental suggestions and commands at least on a subconscious level. Some may hear an audible voice, some an inner voice, while others receive thought injections or impulses. Still others receive visions or visitations. The source may be good or evil. We have to learn to discern and choose which transmissions we will act upon and which we will reject.

The ancients, as recorded in the Bible, received both audio and visual communications from the spirit worlds, as well as actual manifestations. Throughout the Old and New Testaments the priests, prophets, apostles and disciples all had access to inter-dimensional portals. They communicated directly with God. They were able to open portals and travel deep into the spiritual realm, and even to transport themselves instantaneously to distant places on the earth. This is evident, even in the poorly translated English Bibles, and is stated clearly in the original languages of Scripture.

Until recently, the theme of portal travel was relegated to science fiction books and movies. Modern Science now acknowledges that it is a conceivable reality. Physicists have reopened Albert Einstein's unfinished work in the realm of "string theory," which allows for inter-dimensional portals, even time travel.

SOLID ENERGY

Things that appear solid in this physical realm are actually made up of energy. This is a simple fact that we all learned in grade school science class. Everything is made up of atoms, energy, moving at various frequencies depending upon the substance.

The following quotation appears on many websites and is attributed to Albert Einstein,

> Concerning matter, we have been all wrong. What we have called matter is energy, whose vibration has been so lowered as to be perceptible to the senses. There is no matter.

There is a very good chance the quotation is genuine, but whether these are the actual words of Einstein is of little consequence. The important thing is that in the light of quantum physics, it is a true statement.

Everything that exists is manifested as the result of vibrations of pure energy. All matter is comprised of tiny vibrating strings of particles. Different wavelengths determine what substances we see and feel. What is manifest to our senses visually and audibly is minuscule compared to all the invisible waves around us. Physicists are now telling us all those invisible strings make up other dimensions and even parallel universes. There are other realms co-existing with us simultaneously in the same space. According to the model it is theoretically possible to create a wormhole portal in the fabric of time and space through which we could physically travel. They say we could step into a portal in one city and step out in another. We could travel to a distant point on this Earth, or to another world in another dimension, perhaps even another time. This is Science speaking. Quantum physicists are working on this right now.

A number of instances of portal travel were actually recorded thousands of years ago in the Bible. Here are just a few, Genesis

28:11-22; 32:24-30; Exodus 24:9-11 (sapphire); 24:15-18; Ezekiel 1:1-ff; 37:1-ff; Acts 7:54-56; 8:26-39; Revelation 4:1-ff.

COLLIDING REALMS

The heavenly kingdom is with us. We exist in the same space. God, the angels and demons are all right here among us. The spirit world exists at a frequency undetectable to our physical senses. At times, and in certain places, people are able to see angels or demons. Frequencies may shift allowing them to temporarily become visible to us. Some people seem to be more sensitive to the vibrations and are able to see these manifestations when the rest of us cannot. Sometimes special film or electronic cameras are able to bridge the gap and capture images of the otherwise invisible world. Beyond our realm of time, the past, present and future may all exist simultaneously, at various levels within parallel universes.

Portals have been known to open randomly in different locations on the Earth, most notably in the Bermuda Triangle and the Devil's Sea. They have been reported in many places, but are unpredictable and uncontrollable. Sometimes people are transported to another place on Earth, and have to make their way back home. Other people go apparently into different dimensions, sometimes returning with stories of angels or demons in another world. Some report various strange ordeals, even abductions. Others have altogether lost their sanity, while some just never return at all.

We have lost the key that is necessary to gain access to enter in and out of portals freely. We have no control over them. The answer is in heavenly vibrations. Yesu Christ said that his followers would be able to come in and out of the portal at will (John 10: 1-9). He scolded the religious leaders for taking away the key of knowledge (*gnosis*: knowing) so they could not enter in, and for preventing others who might have entered (Luke 11: 52).

Over 35 years ago, I visited the Robinsonville Marian chapel with one of my brothers (I was Catholic at the time). He walked the grounds while I was in the chapel praying. Deep in prayer, I completely lost track of my surroundings. Suddenly I was outside behind the chapel. I could not see my body but my consciousness was there. With each step I saw my footprints in the grass but could not see my feet. I walked toward the covered crucifix where I stopped to meditate. A little while later, I found myself still in the chapel praying. For a brief moment I was surprised and shocked to find myself there, wondering what had just happened.

Shortly, my brother and I reunited. He was very excited as he related his experience. While walking the grounds, he said, he was going toward the crucifix when suddenly he noticed footsteps imprinting the grass in front of him. He watched as the footprints walked step by step to the crucifix and stopped before it.

He had actually seen my footprints appear in the grass before him, but did not see me. I knew that I was there but could not see my own body. At that time neither of us knew exactly what had happened, only that it was something miraculous and mysterious. We did not know why it happened or what it meant. In recent times, God has been leading me in the investigation and study of portals, in both spiritual and secular writings. Now it seems apparent that we witnessed some type of portal experience that was probably triggered by my meditation. My prayer was silent, so it was something internal that altered my frequency and placed me in the spirit realm. I had not completely entered the spirit realm, because I still saw this physical world, and although my body was not visible, my feet still imprinted the tangible grass blades. No one was in the chapel at the time, so whether my physical body disappeared while I was outside, we will never know.

PORTAL OF HEAVEN

In Old Testament times portals were abundant. Jacob's portal and stairway to heaven opened to him in a dream. The stones that were set by his head generated a frequency that caused him to enter the spirit realm in his sleep. He entered another dimension where he saw a ladder, a spiral staircase, with its top reaching to heaven, and angels ascending and descending on it. Yahweh stood above it and spoke to him (Genesis 28: 12-13). Jacob awoke frightened, and exclaimed, "How dreadful is this place! This is none other but the house of God, and this is the portal of heaven." (Genesis 28: 17). He set up a pillar of the stones that had activated the portal frequency around his head while he slept. On top of the pillar, he placed the capstone ("stone of Asher," האבן אשר; "the stone of fire," אש האבן, i.e. pyra-mid) that was the main generator of the portal frequency. It was apparently a pyramid-shaped stone; probably a crystal that emitted constant energy, and was a pre-figuration symbolic of Christ Yesu, the "chief cornerstone" properly translated the "head," or "top" stone. He is the top-stone that the builders rejected (Psalm 118: 22; 1 Peter 2: 4-7).

The mountaintop is a natural representation of the pyramidal capstone. Yahweh visited Moses through a blazing portal, over a bush on top of the mountain. Moses received a set of plans to build a traveling tabernacle with an inner cubicle that would be called the Holy of Holies and the Oracle. This special room housed the Ark of the Covenant. This was the most powerful instrument in the world.

When the ark interacted with the circuitry of interconnected gemstones on the breastplate of the high priest, the Holy of Holies was energized. It was a portal of heaven. The first-Century historian, Josephus, recognized this when he referred to it as, "a heaven peculiar to God." He knew that when the high priest interacted with the ark something miraculous happened. The Holy of Holies was transformed, and was no longer just a room in the tabernacle. The physical and spiritual realms united in the same space. The invisible came into view. The cubicle became the throne room of Yahweh.

God came to earth while simultaneously the high priest found himself standing in heaven. At that moment heaven and earth were one.

The power of the Ark of the Covenant energized and amplified the frequencies of the breastplate stones, altering the vibrations in the cubicle and opening the portal.

God is the highest form of energy, and the source of all energy in the universes. God calls himself a rock. It is he that set up the frequencies in the stones and in everything else that exists. Stones are an important source of stored frequencies. Modern technology has devised many important uses for the frequencies held within crystals. These natural vibrations are energy from God.

The same frequencies that emanated from the stone of Asher, the "stone of fire" on the breastplate, are what activated and opened a spiritual portal for Jacob. He built an obelisk pillar and placed the miraculous capstone on it, proclaiming, "This stone …will be God's house." (Genesis 28: 22).

The stones on the mountaintop created portal frequencies when Moses first saw the light of God.

When the first covenant was given, Yahweh's voice sounded as the voice of the shofar, ram's horn trumpet. There was fire, smoke, lightning and thunder, and the whole mountain quaked greatly. The frequencies on the mountaintop were altered and a portal opened.

God instructed Moses in the proper construction of a mobile tabernacle portal, through which he would funnel his power and presence into this physical world. It was an assemblage that could be carried by the Israelites on their journeys through the wilderness. The structure was a pre-figuration and typology of the true temple portal, Yesu Christ, the great high priest.

Yesu was the word made flesh, to tabernacle among us (John 1: 14). He is the temple of God, torn down and rebuilt again. He said, "I am the portal: by me if any man enter in, he shall be saved, and shall go in and out, and find pasture." (John 10: 9). The proper entrance is through Yesu. He said no man cometh to the father but through me. Entering by another way is possible but the end may be tragic.

At times we are able to open spiritual portals. Why do we not have control over physical portals also? We need to rediscover Yesu's key.

Christ walked through solid walls in his physical body. He was able to make himself invisible, and to travel instantaneously through time and space, because he was master of the portal (a few examples, (Luke 4:28-30; John 6:19-25; 20:26).

ENERGIZE THE PORTAL – RIVER OF LIGHT

We are deep into the project of reconstructing the Biblical and scientific data necessary to reactivate the Portal of Heaven, and to witness first-hand the awesome glory of the almighty Yahweh as he once again descends in the whirlwind pillar of cloud and fire. God's people were able to travel the portals 2,000 years ago, and we will do it again.

The unchangeable God Almighty is pure energy. The light that emanates eternally from this source, according to ancient mysticism, is what created all that exists. Scripture says that light is Yesu Christ, the foundation stone. The mystics have believed there is a heavenly tabernacle, patterned after the tree of life and tree of knowledge of good and evil. Within the holy of holies is a foundation stone from which roots and branches reach out as paths or rays of "light" (energy) to supply the electrical sustenance necessary for all existence, heavenly and earthly.

I have seen a River of Light. It is the same type of light that flows from before Yahweh's throne, only on a small scale, that God allowed me to see. It flowed from the side of a gigantic Van de Graaff Generator we had made to simulate the power coming from the Ark of the Covenant. There was some leakage around the base of the generator's globe, where a half-million volt stream of light was flowing to the discharge wand. My son and I said, almost simultaneously, "The light is flowing like water." There was a six-inch diameter flow of light that reached downward and then curved back up at a 90 degree angle to the discharge wand thirteen inches away. You could actually see the movement of the light resembling the look of swift moving water. It looked like water blasting from the end of a fireman's hose. Within this river of light were scattered sparks, like sparkles on the water. Occasional lightning bolts shot forth within the flow. It was a spectacular display of awesome beauty and power.

When Scripture says a "fiery stream" issued forth from before God's throne, the Hebrew words of Daniel are actually, "river of light." At the time the Bible was translated into English this Hebrew term probably seemed unimaginable. It is easy to picture a stream of fire shooting out, like some kind of a flame-thrower, but who could visualize a river of light? Unless I had seen it with my own eyes, coming from the generator, I could never have imagined such a thing. The scientists of our time must also have seen this in their experiments. It is an awesome sight for anyone to see. But finding the reference hidden within the wording of Scripture, made it even more awesome, just to realize we were viewing a small model of the actual River of Light that flows from the presence of Yahweh.

Daniel saw the "Ancient of days," upon his fiery throne of light. "His throne was like sparks of light, its whirlwinds of fiery-light. A **river of light** flowed in the presence from before him" (Daniel 7: 9-10).

Yahweh also opened a portal of heaven for the Apostle John to view the things recorded in the book of Revelation. John saw the throne of light and the luminous river of life.

> After this I looked, and, behold, a *portal* was opened in heaven: and the first voice which I heard was as it were of a trumpet [*shofar*: ram's horn] talking with me; which said,

Come up hither, and I will show thee things which must be hereafter.

And immediately I was in the spirit: and, behold, a throne was set in heaven, and one sat on the throne.

And he that sat was to look upon like a jasper and a sardine stone: and there was a rainbow round about the throne, in sight like unto an emerald.

And round about the throne were four and twenty seats: and upon the seats I saw four and twenty elders sitting, clothed in white raiment; and they had on their heads crowns of gold.

And out of the throne proceeded lightnings and thunderings and voices: and there were seven lamps of fire burning before the throne, which are the seven Spirits of God.

And before the throne there was a sea of glass like unto crystal... (Revelation 4: 1-6).

And I saw a throne of great *brilliant light* (Greek, *leukon*), and him that sat on it, from whose face the earth and the heaven fled away; and there was found no place for them. (Revelation 20: 11).

And he shewed me a *luminous* (Greek, *lampron*) river of water of life, clear as crystal, proceeding out of the throne of God and of the Lamb. ...

And they shall see his face; and his name shall be in their foreheads.

And there shall be no night there; and they need no candle, neither light of the sun; for the Yahweh God giveth them light: and they shall reign for ever and ever. (Revelation 22: 1, 4-5).

The river of light is the life-force of men (John 1: 1-14). We run on electrical impulses. If something interrupts or impedes our electrical circuits we are in trouble. Without electricity we die. In Scripture, water, fire and light symbolize the regenerating life of the Holy Spirit.

God is pure unfathomable energy, emanating from an infinite eternal source, endlessly creating and recreating within himself. He is all the energy in string theory and the intelligence that keeps the vibrational frequencies in tune to the perfect harmonic symphony of the universes. He is all the light of every star and sun, dwelling in the vast unending darkness of "empty" space, and all the hidden energy pulsating in every other dimension. He was the flash that brought it all into being and he will be the final unifying flash that completes his plan.

He is the fiery whirlwind portal that went before the Israelites to guide them through the wilderness. Everywhere he appeared he brought fire and light. To some it was destruction. To others it was Life.

Right now, we cannot walk through walls, and we cannot travel the fiery whirlwinds to distant places. We do not yet have access to the physical portals that can carry us away and bring us back. But, we can communicate with God in the spirit, and enter the spiritual portals of heaven. We can feel the real presence of God in his glory. We can feel the healing touch of his Holy Spirit as he communicates directly to our inner being. You are the temple of God. Let the veil be opened.

THE BLUE STAR (SAPPHIRE SPHERE)

In February of 1975, I had realized that every waking moment of my life was filled with activity and yet I was empty. There had to be more to life than what I was experiencing. Life was full of excitement but there had to be more to it than that. I had been running wild for fifteen years, with the outcasts of society. I was proud to be a rebel. As an outlaw biker, steeped in alcohol and drugs, my blurred mode of life was all party time. I had been directly geared to the self-destructive path of hedonism. I did the same unseemly things, day after day, night after night. How senseless? How hopeless? How depressing? (Not just rebels, but people in all walks of life are wandering aimlessly, in autopilot mode, bouncing from one commitment to another, careers, children's events, electronics, hobbies, church and civic groups, etc. Living full lives, but with empty hearts.)

If I were here to just satisfy myself, then my life was senseless. It was time for me to start my search for God and the answers to the riddle of life.

Suddenly I felt a requirement and necessity to seek out the answers, not just for myself, but also for all of humanity. We are all in this together and we need to find out why. I vowed to God that I would do whatever it takes to find the answers and help others. I didn't start with the Church or with prayer. I had been there. I began reading books on the mind and the psychic world. Many experiences I read about had already happened to me, so it was easy for me to believe, and my faith built fast. One of the books I read said that alcohol does more damage to the mind and body than any drug. Immediately I began complete abstinence.

I knew that God was working a miracle because I had no withdrawal symptoms. For fifteen years I had been a chronic alcoholic. It even destroyed my marriage. I was helpless to stop. Many times I tried and failed. This time was different. The desire for alcohol and drugs was completely removed and I knew I was cured.

With all the changes in my life, I was looking for some type of exercise to get back in shape. I found Yoga to be a very relaxing exercise that brings you closer to God, through helping you to know your own body. Through my studies I became interested in meditation. I started experimenting. Within a few weeks, I had my first really sensational experience.

After a few minutes of meditating everything blackened and I was staring into a deep Void. Suddenly, I saw a blue light far off in the distance, like a star. The light was coming toward me, getting closer and closer. Soon it was about fifteen feet from me, a beautiful blue in color, like blue glass, but glowing like a star. It was about the size of a grapefruit. It hovered nearby (about three feet away) for a short time, and when it was gone, I felt that God had touched me. I felt relaxed and peaceful, and this is what started the change in my life from an earthbound existence to a spiritual one.

I had entered a spiritual portal, but did not realize it at the time. I had seen the blue light, the sapphire sphere. Was it God? Was it an angel? I did not know. All I knew was that it was a special experience, and I wanted more.

STUMBLING IN THE LIGHT

Needing spiritual nourishment but not knowing where to turn, I was at a loss. Then I recalled an advertisement, promising cosmic consciousness through the secret order of the Rosicrucians. I was compelled to join them, and learned many wonderful secrets (they do hold many secrets of the Universe, but not the knowledge of salvation). After a time, I began to see their plot and their folly. It was a little scary because by then I had heard that it was easy to get in, but that you couldn't get out. Fortunately, I was not too deep yet and was able to quietly retreat and withdraw without making any waves.

I have experienced mental telepathy, *deja vu* and clairvoyance. These mental powers can exist through God, but may result as communications from angels, both good and evil. Some evil angels are designated as such because Yahweh has specifically assigned them to commit evil deeds, or to deceive certain people. Other evil angels have chosen to be evil. They are the rebels we call demons and devils. Therefore much caution is necessary. Spiritual things are easily misinterpreted so it is important to test everything against the

Scriptures. Bible translations all have some flaws but they can still point us in the right direction. Even an inferior map can get you to the correct destination.

Psychic phenomenon and spiritual powers were something I had never believed in, but now they were a part of me. Knowledge of their real existence made life all the more puzzling and increased my need to find God. I wanted to reach God, to make contact, to learn his will.

I kept meditating, studying literature on psychic knowledge and just experiencing life from day to day. I began to feel an awareness of God all around. I realized that God is in everything, and began to see the beauty in everything. I spent a year being educated by nature itself.

Then I had an urge for even more knowledge, and decided to go back to school. In February of 1976, I enrolled at UW-Green Bay (for just one semester).

THE VISITATION

I was having problems running my business (Bullseye Body Shop and Custom Painting) and going to school at the same time. The tension was really building, and by February 11, it was at its peak.

> In a vision, I found myself at the bottom of a pit. I was stuck belly first in the gooey muck and slime. Satan was on my back sinking me deeper into the filth. I was able to strain my neck upwards and see light at the top of the shaft but I had no hope of reaching it. I remember saying to God, there's no place but hell for a guy like me. I was refusing to pray, feeling that I had mocked God too many times by asking for forgiveness and then committing the same sins over again. But I didn't want to sin, not now that I loved God. I cried, and said, God let me die in the night so I won't have to wake up tomorrow and sin. (*Six Nights Till Morning...* p.265).

That night I knew I had to make a decision. I could continue my own way and suffer the agony and torment of a soul in bondage, or I could surrender my life to God. Something inside told me that if I would surrender all, God would save me from my turmoil. I surrendered.

Before going to bed, I decided to meditate In hopes of relieving some of the tension. While I was trying to meditate, I found it impossible to clear my mind. The cares of the day kept surfacing, and soon I thought of how I hadn't prayed seriously in a long time. Until now my meditations had been lacking something. So I combined my meditation with a simple prayer that I repeated over and over. Within my mind, I followed the life and passion of Christ, from his birth through his crucifixion. I could see that it was I who had condemned him; it was I who spit in his face; it was I who scourged him, tearing his flesh with my sins; it was I who crucified him.

Having been raised Catholic, the Hail Mary was a familiar prayer and the one I had chosen as a mantra (at the time I didn't know prayers to the dead were forbidden by God's Word).

I repeated the words of the prayer over and over. At first, they were just words to me, but before long I could feel them taking on deep meaning. As they became more meaningful I paid closer attention thinking about every word and acknowledging the meaning. The prayer was Marian, but my thoughts were completely on Christ and his sufferings. While I was praying, a strange and wonderfully awesome feeling began to manifest. It was different from anything I had ever felt before. Being ignorant of Biblical truths at that time, I initially thought it was the spirit of Mary visiting me. It was a definite feeling of a presence. I was not alone. This was something new and strange that I did not understand. I was afraid, and although I could have stopped at any time, as the feeling intensified I was compelled to continue. "It was coming closer and closer. I could tell by the feeling I was receiving. I could feel [the] presence getting stronger, and my prayers more meaningful. There was nothing else in my mind…" (Having no Biblical understanding at the time, it was easy to misinterpret this experience as a visitation from Mary, because of the prayer I was using. But actually, the Hail Mary had only acted as a mantra. All my thoughts were on the sufferings of Christ. The presence I felt was really God visiting me in the form of the Holy Spirit. This was later confirmed to me).

> "I burst into tears….It was such a great feeling to be in *the heavenly* presence that I couldn't stop crying. I felt so sorry for my sins that my heart was sinking [I curled into a fetal position on the floor]. Then through an inner voice, *I was* told that my sins were forgiven because I was sorry for them and that I would not want to sin again. At this, I began to feel less sorrowful, but I was still worried about someone else [a brother]. I presented the problem *and said* how worried I was. *An inner voice* told me not to worry, that he would be just fine. Now joy swept through me….I was smiling so hard …and the tears were pouring down my face. Then through this inner voice *I was told to* teach others how to pray so that they also can make contact with the Holy Spirit. I promised that night that I would write a book on how to pray, and that I would do everything possible to teach others."

The inner voice (thought injection) told me to, "*teach others how to pray so that they also can make contact with the Holy Spirit.*" Not so they can make contact with Mary, but with the Holy Spirit. God had touched me. It was the Holy Spirit that communicated with me on that wonderful night. I did not see anyone nor did I hear an audible voice. My false assumption that it was Mary stemmed from the mantra I used. But it was only a mantra that cleared my mind so God could enter. My vision turned to the sufferings of Christ, and how my sins were to blame. Yesu is the Lamb of God who takes away the sin of the world. The presence that visited me was the Holy Spirit, to console me and rescue me from my despair.

Having misinterpreted the experience, I began encouraging others to employ the Hail Mary and the rosary to reach the presence of God. I was zealous for God, but without knowledge, and was ignorantly peddling misinformation, as I soon learned.

This is a common occurrence with people who receive a first touch from God. They feel wonderful and know that something marvelous has happened. Their excitement over the experience just naturally entices them to want to tell about it. In this state of premature witnessing many mistakes are made. Such baby talk is a detriment to the true gospel, but something that all beginners seem destined to fall prey to. It is good for beginners to hold their tongue, but hard to do so. Hopefully we all become enlightened to truth. Hopefully we all learn and mature.

After my first "inner room" experience, I practiced prayer several times daily, morning, evening and in between, for 20 minutes each time. After a month of faithful pursuit, the presence of God finally returned, never to leave again. Actually, he had not left at all; I just could not feel his presence. It was a type of testing period. When I finally pledged to serve him forever, even if I never felt his presence again, no more were the words out of my mouth and his presence returned so magnificently that I had to pull my car off of the road because I could not see through the tears to drive.

As God directed my path, he showed me that prayers should only be addressed to him. As I experimented with prayer/meditation the feeling would be strongest while I addressed God directly. He wants a relationship with us. When I thought that I was ignoring Mary, I would switch my attention to her and the awesome feeling of God's presence would leave. The prayer became dry. But upon shifting my thoughts back to God, the wonderful feeling would return.

He brought me many times into a spiritual portal, to just sit in his presence and absorb his loving kindness.

He is with us all, at all times. When you begin to seek entrance to the Holy of Holies, the portal of heaven, you may find immediate success, or you may find a long hard road necessitating persistent practice. Press on; the reward is worth the pursuit.

Let me share some of the insights that helped me to achieve a personal relationship with the Almighty.

INSIGHTS

Experiencing God through Meditation:

> With all due respect to modern meditators, their stylish techniques of meditation have less to offer in overcoming the limits of life than Christian meditation has been offering for centuries. They are an excellent preparation for prayer, but a poor substitute for it. This is not meant to demean these methods, but rather to encourage Christian users of these techniques to complete their usefulness. They can lead Christians to an atmosphere of prayer that lacks only Christianization to fulfill the measurements of Christian meditation. The demanded daily period of quiet spent in a Comfortable chair can be spent in the same chair while basking in the presence of God. [Transcendental Meditation's] resulting pure awareness of the absence of objects is an open invitation to be filled by the living God, thereby making it an active awareness. Rather than relaxing in a void, there can be a fulfilling discovery of divinity, because man cannot truly enter deeply into himself without simultaneously discovering God. Christian meditation can finish the helpful preface that modern meditation techniques furnish. Christian meditation is transcendental, too, because it, also, 'goes beyond' - right to Our Father who is in Heaven....
>
> Thomas Merton was a Christian master of meditation who lived a contemplative life in American monasteries, but died, in 1968, an untimely death in Bangkok, Thailand, right in the heart of the Orient. Maharishi Mahesh Yogi is an Indian teacher who, no doubt, is the most pervasive personality in the worldwide meditation trend today. I am sure that you will notice that the words of the Western monk complete, rather than contradict, the observations of the Eastern Maharishi: 'Experience In the TM technique shows that...pure awareness...is the essential basic nature of the mind, But since the mind ordinarily remains attuned to the senses...and their monitoring of the external...it

misses or fails to appreciate its own essential nature...' Thomas Merton activates that awareness: '...contemplation reaches out to the knowledge and even the experience of the transcendent and inexpressible God. It knows God by seeming to touch Him. Or rather, it knows Him as if It had been touched by Him...Hence contemplation is a sudden fit of awareness...of being touched by God.'

Although on the surface, life is full of boundaries, deep within, life is unbounded. The inner core of everyone is wholeness, the transcendental, absolute, non-changing, eternal, infinite unboundedness of life. We showed people how to turn their attention within, to experience the unbounded wholeness of life and bring the mind out fully saturated with it, so that they could start to live unboundedness in the field of boundaries.

Merton, in his final talk on prayer in the United States before leaving for Asia and his sudden death there, Christizes that discovery of self: 'In prayer we discover what we already have. You start where you are and you deepen what you already have and you realize that you are already there. We already have everything; but we don't know it and we don't experience it. Everything has been given to us in Christ. All we need is to experience what we already possess.'

The transcendental state of being lies beyond all seeing, hearing, touching, smelling and tasting - beyond all thinking and beyond all feeling. This state of unmanifested, absolute pure consciousness of the being is the ultimate of life. It is easily experienced through the system of transcendental deep meditation. 'In the practice of transcendental deep meditation, a proper thought is selected and the technique of experiencing that thought in its infant states of development enables the conscious mind to arrive systematically at the source of thought, the field of the Being.

Thus the way to experience the transcendental Being lies in selecting a proper thought, and experiencing its subtle states until its subtlest state is experienced and

> transcended. (*Transcendental Meditation*, Allied Publishers Private Limited, 1963)

The proper thought spoken of here has to be God. After all, it is God we are trying to contact; it is God we wish to experience. The technique of experiencing is prayer/meditation.

> We might roam through the whole universe and search every corner of it; we would never come face to face with God, find Him as He is in Himself. He is infinitely above everything we see and hear and observe in the world. We can neither overtake Him, nor fathom Him, nor embrace Him as we do a creature. In order to encounter Him, we must transcend everything, we must go beyond all." (*The Secret Ways of Prayer*, pp.20-21).

We can do this by combining transcendental meditation and prayer.

> How does one meditate? It is very simple. Ideally, the meditator should have a quiet place to sit, by himself or herself, without telephones ringing, children screaming, or dogs barking. He sits in a comfortable position, preferably with head not supported, You give yourself a few moments with your eyes closed to get peacefully settled and then you begin to think of the mantra - to clear the mind of thought and allow your consciousness to descend slowly [*to your core where God dwells*]. Extraneous thoughts may come into your Consciousness, for instance, problems of the day that are unresolved, when you first try to meditate don't worry about that. Your mantra will come back to you easily and without effort. Other times, you may experience a mixture of mantra and thought; sometimes you will experience an absence of thought, a mental void, which is the ideal meditation. It is truly 'transcending.' (*The Transcendental Meditation Primer*, p.17).

The prayer of silence, in the presence of God is an awesome experience of fulfillment and unity. A complete void without God would be a horrifying feeling of emptiness, loneliness and abandonment. Nobody wants to experience that. The void you seek is simply a quieting of the self, to allow the Holy Spirit to reign. When you reach that void, rather than empty, you will be full. The fullness of God will emerge from within and you will be whole.

> Before entering silent meditation, spend some time in preparation. If you want to talk to God about something, now is the time, for in the depths of the inner room there are no words only love. It is a good practice to meditate on the way of the cross, the passion of Christ, in preparation to entering the silent meditation. Read some of the accounts of the sufferings of Yesu Christ (Psalm 22:1-18; Isaiah 53:1-12; Matthew 27:11-54; Mark 15:1-47; Luke 22:63-71; 23:1-56; John 18:3-40; 19:1-42). Ponder these things in your heart. Consider his death, burial and resurrection. He did it all for you. He is ready to visit you as the Comforter (Holy Spirit). When you do enter the inner chambers, you will be greatly rewarded for having first prepared. With some experience, there will be times when no preparation is necessary and in fact, when it would become a hindrance. At those times you can enter directly into the joy and presence of the Almighty. (*Six Nights Till Morning...* p.269).

CHOOSING A MANTRA

An early Christian mantra was simular to the prayer that justified the publican (Luke 18:13-14), "Yesu Christ have mercy on me a sinner." This could be your mantra, or simply, "God have mercy." You could use the Our Father (the Lord's Prayer) or whatever prayer you chose, although shorter mantras are better. A *single* word is best. Non-Christian gurus often give their students mantras consisting of a name of one of the gods of their pagan pantheon. The secret mantra given by the guru is a strange sounding word to the student who may never suspect it to be the name of a foreign god. Beware. Scripture says not to take the name of a strange god upon our lips.

> Buddhist contemplatives are striving to enter the "Nothing", the "Void" which to them is the ultimate truth. To them this nonentity is the sole reality. But, "man

> cannot derive peace and moral purity from the contemplation of nonentity" (*A Philosophy of Form*, p.382).
>
> If you are contemplating God, and the name of Yesu is your mantra, you will drive all extraneous thoughts from your mind, but rather than a void, you will be filled with the presence of God, you will manifest a God-consciousness. This is the ideal meditation. This is the "inner room". (*Six Nights Till Morning...* p.269).

According to the Bible some who enter the portal do so illegitimately. Yesu Christ said he is the portal and we must enter only through him.

> Verily, verily, I say unto you, He that entereth not by the *portal* into the sheepfold, but climbeth up some other way, the same is a thief and a robber. (John 10:1)
>
> This parable spake Yesu unto them: but they understood not what things they were which he spake unto them.
>
> Then said Yesu unto them again, Verily, verily, I say unto you, I am the *portal* of the sheep.
>
> All that ever came before me are thieves and robbers: but the sheep did not hear them.
>
> I am the *portal*: by me if any man enter in, he shall be saved, and shall go in and out, and find pasture.
>
> The thief cometh not, but for to steal, and to kill, and to destroy: I am come that they might have life, and that they might have it more abundantly.
>
> I am the good shepherd: the good shepherd giveth his life for the sheep. (John 10:6-11)
>
> I am the good shepherd, and know my sheep, and am known of mine.
> (John 10:14)

It is obvious that Yesu is the Shepherd of Israel, the tabernacle of God, the Holy of Holies and Portal of Heaven. He is the direct manifestation of Yahweh God. Yesu is the Light that emanates from the Source (see John 1:1-12).

The greatest proclamation in the Torah is the shema, "*Shema Yisrael Yahweh Elohenu, Yahweh Echad*" (Hear O' Israel Yahweh is our God, Yahweh is One). The Father, Son and Holy Spirit are one. That is why Christ could cite the shema (Mark 12:29-ff). The Holy Spirit, the Spirit of God and the Spirit of Christ are synonymous (study Romans 8:1-17, especially note v.9). They are three manifestations or offices but one essence, one spirit. Yahweh is Yesu, and Yesu is Yahweh.

> Behold, God my *Yesu*; I will trust, and not be afraid: for *Yah Yahweh* is my strength and my song; he also is become my *Yesu*.
>
> Therefore with joy shall ye draw water out of the wells of *Yesu*.
>
> And in that day shall ye say, Praise *Yahweh*, call upon his name, declare his doings among the people, make mention that his name is exalted. (Isaiah 12:2-4)
>
> Wherefore God also hath highly exalted him, and given him a name which is above every name:
>
> That at the name of Yesu every knee should bow, of things in heaven, and things in earth, and things under the earth;
>
> And that every tongue should confess that Yesu Christ is Yahweh, to the glory of God the Father. (Philippians 2:9-11).
>
> ...who hath declared this from ancient time? who hath told it from that time? have not I Yahweh? and there is no God else beside me; a just God and a Saviour; there is none beside me.

Look unto me, and be ye saved, all the ends of the earth: for I am God, and there is none else.

I have sworn by myself, the word is gone out of my mouth in righteousness, and shall not return, that unto me every knee shall bow, every tongue shall swear. (Isaiah 45:21-23)

SEEING THE FATHER

The Bible says, "Whosoever denieth the Son, the same hath not the Father: but he that acknowledgeth the Son hath the Father also" (1John 2:23). Yesu said, "I am the way, the truth, and the life: no man cometh unto the Father, but by me" (John 14:6). He also said, "He that hath seen me hath seen the Father" (John 14:9). "I and my father are one" (John 10:30).

In the King James Version of the Old Testament, wherever LORD is in all capitals, it has replaced the Tetragrammaton, יהוה (YHWH) and should be read Yahweh. Most places where salvation refers to Yahweh it contains the name of Yesu (ישו). If it were translated this way, even the blind would see:

> *Yahweh* is my strength and song, and is become my *Yesu*.
>
> The voice of rejoicing and *Yesu* is in the tabernacles of the righteous: the right hand of *Yahweh* doeth valiantly.
>
> The right hand of *Yahweh* is exalted: the right hand of *Yahweh* doeth valiantly.
>
> I shall not die, but live, and declare the works of *Yahweh*.
>
> *Yahweh* hath chastened me sore: but he hath not given me over unto death.
>
> Open to me the *portals* of righteousness: I will go into them, and I will praise *Yahweh*:

> This is the *portal* of Yahweh, into which the righteous shall enter.
>
> I will praise thee: for thou hast heard me, and art become my *Yesu*.
>
> The stone which the builders refused is become the *top* stone of the corner.
>
> This is *Yahweh*'s doing; it is marvelous in our eyes.
>
> This is the day which *Yahweh* hath made; we will rejoice and be glad in it.
>
> *Hosanna*/save now, I beseech thee, O *Yahweh*: *Yahweh*, I beseech thee, send now prosperity.
>
> Blessed be he that cometh in the name of *Yahweh*: we have blessed you out of the house of *Yahweh*.
>
> God is *Yahweh*, which hath shewed us light: bind the sacrifice with cords, even unto the horns of the altar.
>
> Thou art my God, and I will praise thee: thou art my God, I will exalt thee.
>
> O give thanks unto *Yahweh*; for he is good: for his mercy endureth for ever. (Psalms 118:14-29)

Yahweh is become Yesu, the capstone that was rejected. He is the portal into which the righteous (*tsadikim*) shall enter.

HEAVENLY VOWEL NAME

> If one ascends to the spiritual world ...one can say that it consists entirely of vowels. ...one enters a tonal world colored in a variety of ways with vowels.... This is why you will find in languages that were closer to the primeval languages that the words for things of the supersensible

world were actually vowel-like. The Hebrew word *"Jahve"* for example, did not have the J and the V; it actually consisted only of vowels and was rhythmically half-sung.

(*The Inner Nature of Music and the Experience of Tone*, pp.37-38)

Josephus, the First-Century Jewish historian, attested that God's name was written in four vowels upon the miter of the high priest.

As vowels the Y-H-W-H would be vocalized as, *yod* = ee; *he* = ah; *waw* = oo; *he* = eh. As a final letter, *he*, in a feminine name receives an "ah" sound, but in a masculine name it is "eh" or short "e" (*YHWH or YHVH?*, p.2). The sounds of these four vowels are, ee-ah-oo-eh. The first two, ee-ah, are equivalent to the syllable "Yah." The last two, oo-eh, equal the sound "weh," as in wet without the t. When pronounced all together, smoothly, the ee-ah-oo-eh becomes Yahweh.

The Hebrew vowel-letters יהוה, *YHWH*, or in the *King James Version* Bible "the LORD" (in all capitals) should be read Yahweh.

FLOW OF THE BREATH

Because the name consists of pure vowels, there is no obstruction in the throat or mouth so the name is effortlessly pronounced with the flow of the breath. It is a spontaneous action.

The beauty in this *all-vowel* name is that there are no obstructions when enunciating it. When a vowel is articulated there is no obstruction. It comes without hindrance all the way from the diaphragm. When you say Yahweh, ee-ah-oo-eh, it flows effortlessly with the breath. The lips and throat never have to close. The tongue never touches the teeth or the roof of the mouth. If a person had their tongue cut out they could still say the name of Yahweh. Even without lips or teeth the pronunciation would not be impeded. It is essentially a sound that is freely breathed. (*Returning His Name Recovering His Remnant*).

PRAYER BREATHING

The Bible says let everything that has breath praise Yahweh. The name of our God, Yahweh, is a breathable prayer/mantra. Whether your mantra is Yesu or Yahweh, when you know the truth of Oneness, they cannot be differentiated. Yesu is Yahweh the Saviour. Either appellation will bring the same result for those with the proper intent.

With each inhalation say, or think, YAH. Each exhalation should be, WEH. You are breathing the praise/prayer of Yahweh. Just keep repeating the prayer over and over in your mind. This is easy if you are concentrating on your breath and its meaning. Yahweh is the name of God. It means, "He will be, what he will be." When you succeed in driving all other thoughts from your mind, you will be giving God a special place to occupy.

God is in us all, at all times. It just takes some discipline for him to manifest. Our *self* is so big it usually blocks the light. If you do not feel the presence of God it does not mean that God is not in you, but simply that you have not yet made the connection.

MAKE ROOM FOR GOD

"In prayer, it is a matter or knowing whether (and how) we can attach ourselves to God alone, in Himself. The basic requirement for achieving this latter attachment is to cut ourselves off, at least momentarily, from everything that is not God." (*The Secret Ways of Prayer*, p.21).

> He who wants to hear the whisperings of God must grow mute to all other voices. As long as we can still hear the voice of our self-love, we will not be able to perceive the voice of Our Lord." (*Lord Teach Us How to Pray*, p.115).
>
> If, then, I allow myself to be concerned with creatures when I am praying, they are more within me than God is. I am In contact with them and not with God; since God is not one of them, He remains absent from me." (*The Secret Ways of Prayer*, p.21).
>
> "Under the pretext that the things that come to our mind are neither wicked nor forbidden in themselves, we easily believe that we are committing no wrong when we are concerned with them from one end to the other of our prayer. It is this that deludes us. We have never succeeded in putting ourselves in God's presence; between Him and us is a solid wall of attachment to creatures, which diverts us from His love. (*The Secret Ways of Prayer*, p.24).

To lower this wall and make yourself open to God's love, you must learn to clear all other thoughts from your mind. You must make room for God by removing all thought that does not concern him. You cannot expect to crowd him in among your other thoughts and daydreams. If you cannot acknowledge God's importance by allowing him to occupy your entire mind during prayer, then you will not be privileged to experience his presence.

To clear your mind and thus put yourself in a spiritual state, you must first find a quiet place where you can be alone. Later on you will be able to pray anywhere but first you need practice. You must assume a comfortable position. Don't try kneeling at first, wait until you have had some success. You must relax, and kneeling could be a distraction. To help yourself relax, you may want to take four or five deep breaths. This is not necessary, but if you have trouble relaxing, it may help you. Now, just sit back, relax, and think about God. Think of how God created everything, and exists in everything. Think of how he created you, and exists in you. Think of how wonderful it would be to contact him. You can. He created himself within you for this very reason.

GOD WITHIN

"He is not only far away in heaven. He is not only up in the clouds. He is right there beside you. He is within you. 'After all,' says St. Paul, 'He is not far from any one of us; it is in Him that we live and move and have our being.' For, indeed, we are His children." Yesu said, "I am in my Father, and ye in me, and I in you." (John 14:20).

> The Hindu believes that God is within and he goes inward seeking union. The Christian who should really be looking within (you are the temple of God, Christ in you), is usually found praying to God as though he were a million miles away in some far off heaven. (*The Inner Room*, p.263)

The way to God is through Christ (John 14:6) and the way to Christ is through your inner self. He has created himself within you so that he would be there where you can talk to him at any time. You must show God that you are sincere enough to really want to be with him. If you can't convince yourself of your sincerity you surely cannot convince God. Anything you want God to believe you must believe first. If you are not really sorry for your mistakes, God knows, because you know. If you do not really forgive your enemies, God knows. God knows all that you know because he is inside you. He reads your mind from within. Nothing is ever hidden from him.

Yahweh is in you experiencing this world. He sees through your eyes, hears through your ears, and experiences all that your senses detect and transmit. He feels with your emotions, works with your hands, and walks in your shoes.

Even though God is within you, it is not easy to make the first personal contact.

> The beginner will see that nature does not find prayer easy at all, and therefore he must not add to the difficulty by choosing a subject which does not have any attraction for him. For beginners in the way of prayer, God is more a

> God afar off than a God felt to be close to the soul. The soul does not find it easy to hold fast to God. When one has to pay too close attention to the matter to be discussed in a conversation, it is easy to neglect the person with whom one is speaking. (*Lord Teach Us How to Pray*, p.164).

Therefore, it is important to either use a one-word mantra, like YAH-WEH [or Yesu: yay-soo] or choose a prayer with which you are very familiar. Otherwise invent your own simple mantra prayer. This way you can focus on the meaning of the prayer, rather than trying to remember the next word.

> The Lord's Prayer is the most important of all the Christian documents. It was carefully constructed by [Yesu] with certain very clear ends in view...The Great Prayer Is a compact formula for the development of the soul. It is designed with the utmost care for that specific purpose; so that those who use it regularly, with understanding, will experience a real change of soul. It is the change of soul that matters. The mere acquisition of fresh knowledge received intellectually makes no change in the soul. The Lord's Prayer is especially designed to bring this change about, and when it is regularly used it invariably does so. (*Power Through Constructive Thinking*, pp.113-114).

> Our Father which art in heaven, Hallowed be thy name.
> Thy kingdom come.
> Thy will be done in earth, as *it is* in heaven.
> Give us this day our daily bread.
> And forgive us our debts, as we forgive our debtors.
> And lead us not into temptation, but deliver us from evil:
> For thine is the kingdom, and the power, and the glory, for ever. Amen. (Matthew 6:9-13)

> In order to pray well, we must set aside everything which is not God. If we employ formulas, we must never become their dupes, but make use of them in order to penetrate them; and by means of them, to plunge into the depths of the heart of God. This is why it is important to use very simple formulas and particularly consecrated ones like that of the *Pater Noster*, to persevere in them and to repeat them slowly,

pondering every word. With a purity of intention that is as perfect as possible we must desire nothing else but God, His kingdom, His will, the sanctification of His name. When we do that, we are the master of our own prayer; but in that very instant, prayer actually takes possession of us and carries us off to the deep recesses of divine union. (*The Secret of Prayer*, p.35).

A WORD ABOUT TM

Never use transcendental meditation by itself, only combine it with prayer or God-consciousness. When you clear your mind, you are leaving an opening, which can be filled by, good or evil. If you sit with your mind blank, Satan can enter in and use his subtle influence to trick you. Don't give him the chance. Your mind is like a radio receiver ready to pick up signals from the spirit world. So when you meditate, you must always keep God in your mind. Allow God to take over your every thought so that there will be no room for the evil of Satan. Take this journey to heaven. Open the spiritual portal of your mind. You will find yourself at the beginning of a new and rewarding life.

SPELLING OUT BRAINWAVES

In meditation, brain waves change. Brainwaves are frequencies, vibrations. Our brainwaves are a spiritual ladder leading to a spiritual portal.

Brainwaves are categorized and identified by the Greek letters, Beta, Alpha, Theta, and Delta, in this order.

B = *beta* (awake, active)
A = *alpha* (relaxed, meditative)
Θ = *theta* (between wake and sleep, free-flow of ideas)
Δ = *delta* (sleep, dream)

Let's examine these Greek letters, B, A, Θ, Δ.

The Pythagoreans saw the delta-triangle as a portal of divine manifestation. This correlates perfectly to the triangular pyramidal stone that transmitted a portal frequency for Jacob as he slept. His brainwaves entered the delta or doorway state where Yahweh chose to reveal a heavenly vision. Jacob saw the angels ascending and descending the stairway to heaven.

Examining the remaining brainwave designations as an anagram, the word we see is **BAΘ** (*bath*). This may be a reference to the Greek word *bathos* (less the inflection): "depth, profundity; the interior of a house." This is very fitting, since Scripture tells us we are the temple and tabernacle of God. *Bath* is also an abbreviation for *bathron*: "step, stair; threshold; ladder." Thus, the Greek anagram **BAΘ** (*bath*) signifies, "an interior stairway/ladder."

The delta is a door or portal. So, **BAΘ-Δ** (*bath-d*) would signify *an interior ladder to the portal*, or, *a portal and ladder inside of you*. This is exactly what Jacob experienced and envisioned when he was compelled to exclaim, "This is none other than the house of God and the portal of heaven." (Genesis 28:17). He referred to it as "dreadful"; he knew this was more than an ordinary dream.

All four brainwaves are present at all times, although one state always predominates. The different waves are the rungs of the ladder. The complete interior ladder is always there, we are simply ascending or descending.

An interesting thing happens when we translate the designated Greek letters of the brainwaves into Hebrew characters.

B = ב = *beth* (B)
A = א = *aleph* (A)
Θ = ת = *tau* (T)
Δ = ד = *daleth* (D)

BATD (ב, א, ת, ד) if read from right to left, as Hebrew does, two interpretations are possible, "religion/law of the father," or, "door of longing." But if we read from left to right, as with Greek and English, the translation and interpretation correlates closely to what we have already found. The two center letters, *AT* (תא) are Hebrew for "you." These two letters are also an anagram, *Aleph-Tau*, meaning, "the First and the Last," i.e. the Creator (*aleph-tau* are the first and last letters of the Hebrew alphabet). The D (ד) in Hebrew is *daleth*, which actually means "door." The letter *beth*, as a prefix, means "in." *BATD* (דתאב) is interpreted as, "in you, a door/portal," i.e. "a portal in you." It could also be, "a portal in Aleph-Tau," i.e. "a portal in God."

The brainwave anagram in Greek implies, "*a portal and ladder inside of you.*" The Hebrew rendering signifies, "*a portal in you/a portal in God.*" This marvelous reality reveals the ingenious plan of the Creator to make himself always accessible to his people.

Yahweh has created himself in man. God is manifested in his creation. He is in you and you are in him. You and God are occupying the same space at the same time. The portal in you is the portal in God. You are the tabernacle. When the portal inside of you is activated, you are (as Josephus stated) "a heaven peculiar to God." Peculiar means "private property." You are Yahweh's private property, his acquisition. Scripture calls us "a peculiar people."

> To whom coming, as unto a living stone, disallowed indeed of men, but chosen of God, and precious.
>
> Ye also, as lively stones, are built up a spiritual house, an holy priesthood, to offer up spiritual sacrifices, acceptable to God by Yesu Christ.
>
> Wherefore also it is contained in the scripture, Behold, I lay in Sion a chief corner stone, elect, precious: and he that believeth on him shall not be confounded.
>
> Unto you therefore which believe he is precious: but unto them which be disobedient, the stone which the builders disallowed, the same is made the head of the corner.

> And a stone of stumbling, and a rock of offence, even to them which stumble at the word, being disobedient: whereunto also they were appointed.
>
> But ye are a chosen generation, a royal priesthood, an holy nation, *a peculiar people*; that ye should shew forth the praises of him who hath called you out of darkness into his marvelous light;
>
> Which in time past were not a people, but are now the people of God: which had not obtained mercy, but now have obtained mercy. (1Peter 2:4-10).

DARK NIGHT OF THE SOUL

The contemplative speaks of the dark nights through which the soul must pass before reaching divine union with the Creator. The soul must empty itself of all things and pass through a dark and dry land to reach the presence of God. Saint John of the Cross speaks thus:

> A man makes room for God by wiping away all the smudges and smears of creatures, by uniting his will perfectly to God's; for to love is to labor to divest and deprive oneself for God of all that is not God. When this is done the soul will be illumined by and transformed in God. (*The Collected Works of St. John of the Cross*, p.117)

He says the soul must be emptied of all supernatural and natural "imaginative visions". "For example: the imagining of Christ crucified, or at the column, or in some other scene; or of God seated upon a throne with resplendent majesty...or the picturing of any other human or divine object imaginable." (*ibid.* p.137). The soul will have to abandon these images and "leave this sense in darkness if it is to reach divine union." Saint John of the Cross continues by reasoning that the imagination cannot fashion anything beyond which it has experienced through the exterior senses:

> He will not acquire this spiritual nourishment through the labor of his imagination, but by pacifying his soul, by leaving it to its more spiritual quiet and repose.
>
> The more spiritual a man is, the more he discontinues trying to make particular acts with his faculties, for he becomes more engrossed in one general, sure act. Once the faculties reach the end of their journey, they cease to work, just as a man ceases to walk when he reaches the end of his journey. If everything consisted of going, one would never arrive
>
> It is sad to see many disturb their soul when it desires to abide in this calm and repose of interior quietude, where it is filled with the peace and refreshment of God....Since these individuals do not understand the mystery of that new experience, they imagine themselves to be idle and doing nothing. Thus, in their struggle with considerations and discursive meditations they disturb their quietude.
>
> The advice for these individuals is that they must learn to abide in that quietude with a loving attentiveness to God and pay no heed to the imagination and its work. (*ibid*. p.139).
>
> When the spiritual person cannot meditate, he should learn to remain in God's presence with a loving attention and a tranquil intellect, even though he seems himself to be idle. For little by little and very soon the divine calm and peace with a wondrous, sublime knowledge of God, enveloped in divine love, will be infused into his soul. (*ibid*. p.149).

Yes, to find true rest one must pass through great darkness; to find light one must search the night. God is light but his dwelling place is in the thick darkness (Exodus 20:21; Deuteronomy 5:22-23; Psalm 97:2). "The light shineth in the darkness; and the darkness grasped it not" (John 1:5). "He made darkness his secret place; his pavilion round about him were dark waters and thick clouds of the skies" (Psalm 18:11).

> You can compare the depth of the spirit to the ocean depths. Our moods are constantly changing, just as the surface of the ocean. A little deeper the dimly lit ocean waters are moved by powerful currents. Lower still, there is the "darkness and calm of the profoundest deeps". In the depths of being there

> is calmness. "As the eye of contemplation sinks into this central depth it is lost in its darkness, as the sunlight fails to pierce to the ocean floor." (*A Philosophy of Form*, pp.421-422).

When the soul is held fast by the divine Action, she is receiving the action which in at the same time is absolute rest because it is without movement, eternally concentrated in itself, the...motionless activity; The perfect Resting-Activity or Active-Rest of God...The Divine Energy, being without admixture of potency or matter, is identical with its Form. Since, therefore, in her supreme union with God, the soul receives the Form-Energy which is His Being and Life, in her contemplation of his Form she partakes of the reposeful Energy or active Repose which in Himself is identical with the Form she contemplates. (*ibid*. p.407).

FEELING THE PRESENCE OF GOD

One of the first things to be instructed in prayer is to place yourself in the presence of God. That does not mean to pretend that you are with God but that you can actually feel God's presence. When you place yourself in his presence you do not have to pretend to be with him, you are with him. You are always with him; you just do not always feel it. Apostle Paul said, "...he be not far from every one of us: For in him we live, and move, and have our being." (Acts 17:27b-28a).

When you succeed in removing all extraneous thoughts from your mind so that God alone is there, you will actually feel his presence. There will be no more doubting.

> Gradually this prayer, in which my heart speaks to God without the noise of words, flows into complete silence. In the beginning, in a certain manner, the soul alone was the actor, and the Lord [Yahweh] was the non-actor, the silent one. Now the roles are reversed. The Lord emerges ever more from out of His kindness. He becomes the actor, and I become the non-actor, the silent one. Considered from my point of view, up to now I moved laboriously toward the

> Lord. Now I am the one who is at rest while the Lord is in pursuit of me. (*Lord Teach Us How to Pray*, p.188).
>
> When this contact is accomplished you will feel the Holy Spirit inside of you. Warmness will be felt from within. Your feelings will become much more acute, and you will know that God is with you. "The soul and the heart become completely warm and hot in the presence of God, and retain for a long time an afterglow." (*You Can Actually Be With God*, p.34).

I have felt this warmth of God many times. On one occasion, I was outdoors on a cool, damp day, sitting with my eyes closed, praying to God. I could feel His presence. I was bathed in such warmth that I had to open my eyes to see if the sun had come out. It was just as dismal as ever. I closed my eyes again to bask in the presence of God. Immediately, the warmth returned. It was the warmth that comes with the Holy Spirit.

You can bask in the presence of God. It is a conscious choice that you must decide upon. It is a glorious choice that will change your world. Will you admit that God is waiting inside of you? Do you have the courage to seek Him?

It takes work on your part and dedication. It also takes humility and the surrender of self along with repentance, i.e. a change of heart and mind. You have to want to be with God enough to devote some time to Him, even if it is only ten or fifteen minutes a day. Prayer is not easy and it is going to take practice. If you do not succeed the first few times you try, don't give up. It is all a test. Keep trying, you can do it. Don't be afraid to surrender to God. You will not lose your free will. He will not make a puppet out of you. Don't be afraid to place yourself in his presence. You are part of God. You will feel the magnificence and the glory of God because you have come to him and you are one. "Every one that asketh receiveth; and he that seeketh findeth; and to him that knocketh it shall be opened." (Luke 11:10).

ONCE YOU REACH GOD DO NOT SLACK OFF

After you have felt God's presence, you will want to be with Him as often as possible. If you find it seemingly impossible to make a second contact, you may begin to wonder if he will come again or if he has just shown himself to let you know that he is there. This is a test of your perseverance.

> If we experience a great pleasure as some times happens, an agreeable and intimate pleasure during prayer, we no longer know very clearly why we are praying. We do not know whether we are praying to God in order to draw nearer to Him or for our own pleasure and personal satisfaction. Joy in prayer can be sweet to the heart. It consoles us for many of the sacrifices made. But when prayer offers us no tangible satisfaction, and when we find that prayer engenders only a feeling of aridity and a kind of dark despair but we persist in prayer nevertheless, searching for God alone across this wasteland, rejecting even our own bitter sadness, then we are quite sure that we are actually praying to God in order to find Him. For no earthly personage could impose on us such a harsh and desolate period of waiting. We would never endure it save for the hope that God, the presence of God, is at the end of our long vigil. (*The Secret Ways of Prayer*, p.29).

After my first experience, I prayed day and night. My heart ached for God. I was happy with the experience I'd had, but was yearning for another. I began to wonder what I was doing wrong, but I kept on trying. After about a month I was rewarded and once again allowed to feel the presence of the Holy Spirit. Since then, I have felt God's presence almost continually. You also can feel the presence of God. Just practice these methods and you will succeed.

Once you have learned to enter the spiritual portal, do it often. Become a master. Learn to walk in the presence of God.

Yesu said, "God is a spirit and those who worship him must worship him in spirit and in truth." (John 4: 24). We need prayer that takes us to God in the spirit, and we also need truth that sets us free. The study of his word with the guidance and inspiration of the Holy

Spirit will break the bondage of false doctrines and traditions of men. But it is only the start. For every falsehood that God exposes, he reveals a truth. With every revelation, a multitude of questions arise. And with each answered question, new questions are generated. It is an unending learning process. When you start a walk with God it is a lifelong adventure. Don't even think about starting if you are going to look back. Yesu said, "No man, having put his hand to the plough, and looking back, is fit for the kingdom of God." (Luke 9: 62).

~END I~

Part II

STAYING CONNECTED

NAME ABOVE EVERY NAME

"Let this mind be in you, which was also in Christ Yesu: Who, being in the form of God, thought it not robbery to be equal with God: But made himself of no reputation, and took upon him the form of a servant, and was made in the likeness of men:

"And being found in fashion as a man, he humbled himself, and became obedient unto death, even the death of the cross. Wherefore God also hath highly exalted him, and given him a name which is above every name:

"That at the name of Yesu every knee should bow, of *things* in heaven, and *things* in earth, and *things* under the earth; And *that* every tongue should confess that Yesu Christ *is* Yahweh, to the glory of God the Father." (Philippians 2:5-11)

THE NAME OF SALVATION

The name Yesu is said to mean *salvation* or *saviour*. It more fully means *Yahweh Saviour*. "Neither is there salvation in any other: for there is none other name under heaven given among men, whereby we must be saved" (Acts 4:12). His name in the Biblical languages, Greek, Hebrew and Latin, is

Yesu. This was translated in old English and early modern English as Iesu and pronounced yay-soo, just like in the Biblical languages. Over a period of a few hundred years it gradually morphed into the English name Jesus. This removal and replacement of the name Yesu had been prophesied in the Bible. One such reference is found in Jeremiah 11:19, "I was like a lamb or an ox that is brought to the slaughter, and I knew not that they had devised devices against me, saying, Let us destroy the tree with the fruit thereof, and let us cut him off from the land of the living, that his name may be no more remembered." (For detailed information on the etymology and importance of the saviour's name please refer to *The Holy Cipher: Who Changed God's Name?* or, *The End Is Come*, by Norbert H. Kox).

There is a Jewish curse that states, "His name and his memory shall be obliterated." This is undoubtedly related to Jeremiah 11:19, "...that his name may be no more remembered." The curse is represented by the letters YMS or, according to some, YShW, which they associate with the name Yeshu, or Yesu. (*A Speck Of Atlantis-Bimini: The Top Of God's Mountain*, p.33)

Yesu became a curse for us...the letters of his name meaning, "May his name and his memory be blotted out forever," in other words, "May his name be remembered no more." But if the spelling of his name has this meaning then it will never be forgotten, because every time the curse is mentioned, there is his name. It can never be obliterated. The lowliest name of all is the name above every name.

THE INDESTRUCTIBLE NAME

Many Christian scholars believe that the name of Christ in Hebrew was *Yeshua*. But the name which is pronounced Yeshua (yay-shoo-ah, or, y'shua) by Modern Christian scholars is not pronounced that way by the Jews (with few exceptions) in reference to Christ. The final letter, *ayin* (eye-in) represented by ` is not heard in the pronunciation (*Dictionary of the Bible*, p.71, McKenzie). The *ayin* is usually neglected, although it appears in writing (*cf. Beginners' Hebrew Grammar*, Rev. Harold L. Creager, B.D., p.6). An *ayin* at the end of a word does not necessarily change its pronunciation, neither would an *alef* or *he*. Modern Hebrew dictionaries do not even print the *ayin* in the name Yesu, but simply print the three-letter spelling, *yod, shin, waw*.

In his Bible Code book, Scholar and researcher, Jeffrey Satinover, states, "The silent letters in Hebrew are *'aleph'* and *'ayin'*, which can take on any vowel sound. Many words are spelled with them or without them." (*Cracking The Bible Code,* p.312). The "a" vowel of the final syllable in Yeshua is not derived from the *ayin*, but from the deceptive Masoretic points which did not appear before the 8th century AD. "One has to be careful not to grant the same canonical authority to the Masoretes as to Moses and the prophets. Nor should one be too critical of the modern Old Testament scholar who thinks he has just cause to alter one or two of the signs the Masoretes had introduced." (*Do it Yourself Hebrew and Greek: Everybody's Guide to the Language Tools,* p.14:3).

If the *ayin* had been pronounced it could have represented either of two sounds, *g* or *h*, according to various Hebrew Grammars and *Septuagint* study. But in the name which we are scrutinizing, we can be relatively certain that it was ignored or practically silent, because it was not transliterated in the *Septuagint*. A *g*-sound would have called for a Greek rendering of *Iesoug*, which never appears. An *h*-sound, preceded by a vowel, would scarcely be heard and need not appear in transliteration. "*Ayin* is an aspiration midway in strength between *alef* and *he*. We transliterate it by a rough breathing [`], and practically neglect it in pronunciation." (*Beginners' Hebrew Grammar,* p.6). Yesu and Yesuh would be identical in pronunciation. A word can be closed with an unsounded consonant. The "moveable" *ayin* (even when not pronounced, *ayin* is categorized as a *moveable* letter) could be used in closing, the same as a "silent" *alef* or *he*.

In the Talmudic spelling of the same name, the *ayin* has actually disappeared. Rather than YSW` (*yod, shin, waw, ayin*) the name is simply YSW (ישׁו, *yod, shin, waw*). This leaves no reason to doubt the "Yesu" pronunciation. The Talmud refers to him as YSW HNOTSRY (*Yesu ha Notsriy*: Yesu the Nazarene; *Notsriy* also means Christian).

Like the *Jews for Jesus*, Grant Jeffrey and Yacov Rambsel, in their Bible Code books, use the name Yeshua synonymously with Jesus. Grant Jeffrey says Yeshua is "Jesus," and promotes the name Yeshua over the name Yeshu (Yesu) which he insinuates is incorrect. What he does not realize is that the Hebrew/Aramaic three-letter and four-letter spellings of the Saviour's name are pronounced the same, Yesu or Yeshu, not Yeshua. The Bible Code programs all have the three-letter spelling, not the four, in their data bases. All the Hebrew dictionaries have the three-letter spelling also, and not the four-letter spelling. Mr. Jeffrey suggests the name of Yeshu (Yesu) comes from a derogatory acronym, *Yimach Shemo Uzikhro* [or, *yemach shemo vezichro*] "May his name and memory be blotted out" (*The Mysterious Bible Codes*, pp.99-100). The initial letters of these three words, the *Yod Shin Waw* (YSW) do spell the name of Yesu. The curse is actually pronounced with the words *Yemach shemo,* "his name shall be erased." According to *Ben Yehuda's English-Hebrew/Hebrew-English Pocket Dictionary,* the abbreviation for the *yemach shemo vezichro* curse is YMS, *Yod-Mem-Shin,* for *Yemach shemo* (p.xxiii). If a person's name were to be blotted out and remembered no more, it would have to never be written again, otherwise the purpose would be defeated. It would perpetuate that name rather than destroy it. If the YSW acronym were used as an abbreviation for the curse, every time it was written down it would proclaim the name of Yesu. Rather than blot out his name it would actually preserve it. And, if this is the case, his name cannot be obliterated. (*Who Changed God's Name?* pp.40-42; *Masquerade: Antichrist is Here*, pp.54-56).

His name cannot be obliterated. In fact, every time the curse would be pronounced upon someone, their name would be obliterated while simultaneously being overwritten by the name of Yesu (YSW). In a sense, this happens to us. We are cursed because of sin. When we repent and are baptized, Yesu's name is called out over us. We are superimposed by his name and he has become the "curse" for us (Galatians 3:13). "Cursed is everyone that hangeth on a tree" (Deuteronomy 21:22-23). It is only appropriate that the letters of his name, ישו (YSW) would stand as an acronym for the curse.

These letters (ישו) also spell, "his existence." Reversed, they spell, "and gift." The primary meaning of the name Yesu is, "Yahweh the Saviour." The symmetrical analysis of the name, when it is read forward and then backward, says, "His existence and Gift." (*The End Is Come*, p.153; *The Holy Cipher: Who Changed God's Name?*, pp.69-70).

HIS EXISTENCE AND GIFT

Yahweh's *existence and gift* was and is Yesu Christ, the chief cornerstone, the capstone portal of the resurrected living temple of God. In essence Yesu is Yahweh and the "name which is above every name" (Philippians 2:9).

Yesu is the WORD of God. He said, "I am the way, the truth, and the life: no man cometh unto the father but *through* me." His name, which was made a curse by those who cursed him, is the name that is exalted above all other names... (*A Speck Of Atlantis-Bimini: The Top Of God's Mountain,* p.34).

CLOUD OF UNKNOWING

In their desire and quest for peace, the greater portion of mankind has found it to be the illusive butterfly. It flutters its wings and soars beyond their reach just when they were about to grasp it. Isaiah the prophet wrote, "It shall even be as when a hungry man dreameth, and, behold, he eateth; but he, awaketh, and his soul is empty: or as when a thirsty man drinketh; but he awaketh, and, behold, he is faint and his soul hath appetite" (Isaiah 29:8).

For those with a strong desire to meet with God in the spirit, *The Cloud of Unknowing* was written, by an anonymous fourteenth-century English monk attempting to lead beyond all doctrines and theological concepts, beyond all attachments to religious objects, rituals and ceremonies.

The writer says that anyone thinking he could come to contemplation without having first meditated upon his own wretchedness as well as upon the passion of Christ, his kindness, his love, would surely be in error and fail to achieve his purpose but yet for a man or woman who has continued in these meditations for a long time, it is necessary to discontinue them, to hold them down beneath the "cloud of forgetting" if he is ever to pierce the "cloud of unknowing" that is between him and his God.

In Biblical metaphor the cloud is often representative of a portal of Yahweh's presence (Exodus 19:19-20; *cf*. 24:15-18; 2Chronicles 5:13-14; Job 22:13-14; 38:1; 40:6; Ezekiel 10:3-9).

Your prayer shall be your shield and spear, to beat upon the cloud and the darkness, and, to beat down all extraneous thoughts. These thoughts or voices are referred to as "him." Your spear may be the prayer of the publican, "God be merciful to me a sinner," (Luke 18: 13) or just "God have mercy." The shorter prayer is better: "Yahweh," "Yesu," or simply "God."

> A prayer of a single word is best. If any thought should rise up, you will beat "him" down with this word. Even what appear to be holy thoughts could at this time distract you from your goal, just as it would be unlawful and would seriously hinder a man who was sitting in his meditations to turn his attention to his outward bodily works so would it hinder a man undertaking to work in this darkness...if he would let any thought or any meditation of God's wonderful gifts, kindness, and works in any of His creatures physical or spiritual rise upon him to press between him and his God, no matter how holy these thoughts might be, nor how profound, nor how pleasant. (*The Cloud of Unknowing*, p.82).

BREAKTHROUGH

At first this work will seem strenuous but after a while the difficulty will leave. Then you will have little or no work to do for God himself will take over. This may only be for short periods at a time, but you must then allow him to work. "Then will He perhaps sometimes send out a beam of spiritual light piercing the cloud of unknowing that is between you and Him, and He will show you some of His secret ways of which man neither can nor may speak." (*ibid*. p.125).

"Often there will come to us a sweet, joyful sense of the presence. Often our hearts will burn within us as He draws nigh to commune with us as He did with Enoch. When this is in truth the experience of a Christian, there is seen in his life a simplicity, a humility, meekness, and lowliness of heart, that show to all with whom he associates that he has been with [Yesu] and learned of Him." (*Christ's Object Lessons*, pp.129, 13; quoted from, *New Life: Bible Guide*, no.11).

INTO THE INNER ROOM

Prayer is not talking to yourself; it is communion with God. The object is not really to ascend or transcend but rather to descend into the core of your being. When you enter that inner room, you will find perfect peace and tranquility awaiting you there. You must get past the turmoil of the surface and go deep into that place where God secretly awaits to enlighten you. By going inward you cut yourself off, at least temporarily, from the outer or physical world. When you have been successful you will find yourself in a place where you've probably never been before, or only dreamt of, a beautiful place, a peaceful place. This is the inner room. It is nowhere and yet it is everywhere. It is inside yet it seems to engulf the entire universe. It is a secret place where lovers meet. It is a place of refreshing.

> Yahweh is good unto them that wait for him, to the soul that seeketh him. It is good that a man should both hope and quietly wait for the salvation of Yahweh. (Lamentations 3:25-26).

Do not be impatient. When you reach the inner room, don't allow Satan to deceive you into thinking there is nothing there for you. He will want you to think the room is empty so you leave and never return. But wait; Say, "I won't leave until God visits me." Scripture says, "They that wait upon Yahweh shall renew their strength." Do not strain to see something or hear some thing, this would involve the physical senses. We want to empty the room of all seeing, hearing and reasoning. You cannot find the presence of God through your own reasoning and mental effort. He must be accepted and received as he is, through the darkness of faith. Once you are in his presence he may choose to bestow any number of blessings upon you.

The inner room of your bodily temple is the Holy of Holies and spiritual portal of heaven.

CLEANING HOUSE

If you find the room full of junk (distractions) you will have to clear it out. If the junk keeps piling up, don't be discouraged, keep cleaning it out. Once in a while you will get a break. As you persist, the cleaning will become easier. You will be able to spend more time at Yesu's feet and less time cleaning house.

Don't be deceived into believing that you have reached the consummation when you have reached the inner room. You must worship God in "spirit and in truth." You need to study the Word of God so that you can "try the spirits," or someday you may find yourself within the inner room, entertaining Satan who is disguised as an "angel of light."

Yesu said, "they shall cast out devils in my name; they shall speak with new tongues" (Mark 16:17). If you suspect the enemy may be lurking, you can say, "Get out of this room devil, only Yesu is welcome." And you can use the name of Yesu to beat him down and tread him under.

SPIRIT BAPTISM

When you have been to the inner room, bathed in the presence of YHWH, there is a desire to come forth and express what you feel. Words are inadequate. When you bring forth this prayer "which cannot be uttered," it will be expressed in an angelic tongue. At this time it is the "Spirit which maketh intercession" in a language that "no man understandeth" (1Corrinthians 13:1; 14:2; Romans 8:26-27). This is identical with the apostolic "upper room" experience of the day of Pentecost. The upper room was an inner room, where all were gathered in one accord when the Spirit came as a rushing wind (*pneuma*: "spirit") and filled the whole house and all those within it (Acts 2:1-4).

You must put your inner room in order and all thoughts in one accord. And suddenly there will come from heaven a mighty rushing Spirit, which will sweep through the room, thrilling you with the feeling of ecstasy.

Yesu said, "The wind [Spirit] blows where it will, and you hear the sound of it...so it is with everyone that is born of the Spirit" (John 3:8). When a person is born of the Spirit there will be a sound, a sign, a manifestation that can be heard even as the wind can be heard. On the day of Pentecost when they were all filled with the Holy Spirit, they were heard speaking in other tongues, there was a sound, an audible manifestation of the Spirit. When the same Spirit rushes through your temple filling the inner room with his sweet presence, allow him to outwardly manliest himself through the speaking of tongues. This is not to say that you will abandon the work of the inner room, or the rest that is there; sometimes you will enter in and bask in the refreshing quietude of the interior presence of God, and other times you will emerge and come forth speaking in a heavenly language, which alone can express the perfect union that has taken place. The contemplatives refer to this union, which renders the soul "habitually conscious of God," as the "mystical marriage." New tongues are the language of the Bride of Christ.

A person can receive the baptism of the Holy Spirit without first meditating or contemplating, without previously entering the inner room. The only Biblical prerequisite is that he repent, turn, change. Repent of sins simply means turn away from mistakes. The union, which for the ascetics and mystics has taken a lifetime of self-denial, can be reached instantly, with the right mindset. The gift of the Holy Ghost is free. It does not have to be labored for. A person receives in faith; In faith he speaks in tongues. When someone prays or sings in an unknown tongue, his mind is cleared of all extraneous thoughts, for his understanding is unfruitful (unless God provides an interpretation). The thought process is not involved in the speaking of tongues since it is the Spirit that giveth utterance. The mind may still try to wander; it is our nature. The words spoken are as the sword of the Spirit, and should strike down all intruding thoughts. Through the intercession of the Holy Spirit entrance is gained to the inner room. Many people today are receiving the Holy Spirit and speaking the language of the bride. They have access to the inner room, yet the majority of these have never stopped to listen for the voice of the Bridegroom. They always labor to caress the Bridegroom and never wait for him to return his affection.

In the original language of the Scriptures the word baptize signifies a washing, or a bath, by immersion. The baptism of the Holy Ghost is an immersion or a bathing in the Spirit. In the "mystical marriage" described by the contemplatives, "This most powerful and infinite Deity bathes the center of the soul…he bathes the entire soul and body….The entire being is bathed by the Being of God; while this Divine ray of the Deity endures it fills the entire soul and body." (*A Philosophy of Form*, p.427).

> To say that we don't need the baptism in the Holy Spirit is the same as to say that we don't need to be cleansed, immersed in, and saturated by God's Truth, nor do we need the fullness of His power operating in and through us. (*Power in Praise*, p.49).

Can you receive the baptism of the Holy Ghost without speaking in tongues? Can you be the Bride of Christ without speaking in tongues? If the answer were yes, it would not be without consequences. To refuse or resist speaking in tongues would be to hinder the work of the Spirit. For any relationship to function properly, there must be a sharing and an equal participation. A marriage where one partner puts forth all the effort and does all the talking is not a perfect and mutual union. You must keep silent at times so that the Bridegroom can speak to you, but you must also speak to him at times in the language of the Bride.

When you pray outwardly among others (unless in a praise service among believers) it should be in your native language, that they may understand. But when you enter the secret chambers let it be intimate, speak the language that the Bridegroom has given you which "no man understandeth," and also take time to be silent as he communicates to you. Sometimes you speak. Sometimes he speaks. Other times you are both silent. You absorb the light in a silence more powerful than words.

Some people fear the baptism of the Holy Ghost because of all the propaganda against speaking in tongues. Things that people do not understand they often want to destroy. Christ-loving-people battle against the Holy Spirit because they are ignorant of his workings. They actually blaspheme the Holy Ghost by attributing his workings to the devil. If left unrepented, this is the unpardonable sin (Matthew 12:24, 31).

CRITICAL ANSWERS

Let me answer some of the accusations against speaking in tongues: It is not a possession but a yielding to the moving of the Holy Spirit. The actual speaking in tongues begins with an operation of the will. You must choose to speak. If you keep your mouth shut nothing will come out. You must use your lips, tongue and vocal cords to produce the sound. It will be your voice but like the Scripture says, the Holy Spirit of God gives the utterance. Just begin to speak in faith and whatever syllables or sounds come forth will be an expression of the Spirit within. There is nothing to memorize or learn so you can't make a mistake, you can't say anything wrong.

While speaking in tongues, you don't lose consciousness or go into a trance; a person is completely conscious and in full control (1Corinthians 14:32). He is rational and is aware of what he is doing. He can stop at any time he chooses or shift from tongues back to his native language. A person does not have to work himself up, or pray for a long period of time, or go into a trance or ecstasy. He does not become possessed by a spirit which takes over his body. It is a simple yielding to the Spirit of Yahweh. One may become very emotional while speaking in tongues, although it is possible to speak quite calmly.

If you do not believe in it, then it simple is not for you. It is only for believers. If you do believe but have not yet experienced it, all you need to do is ask.

In the traditional manner of prayer one is seldom, if ever, ever, able to experience the direct presence of God in the soul. Anyone who is willing to exercise self-denial and discipline, can, with the proper instruction and practice feel the ecstatic joy of the accomplished mystic.

CHURCH OF THE SPIRIT

The early church father, Tertullian, "...held that there exists an internal 'Church of the Spirit,' which he contrasts with the 'Church of the bishops.'" All Spirit-filled believers he considered to have special powers (*New Catholic Encyclopedia*, vol.13: p.1022). Tertullian believed in tongues and prophecy, and that Spirit-filled individuals had exclusive communication with the Almighty God.

Another early church father, Irenaeus, wrote, "We hear many brethren who have prophetic gifts and they speak in all sorts of languages through the Spirit. (*The Phenomenon of Pentecost*, p.51). Still another, Justin Martyr, "...tells how the gifts of the Spirit were in operation in his day" (*ibid.* p.52). In the fourth century Saint Augustine said, "We still do what the apostles did when they laid hands on the Samaritans and called down the Spirit on them it is expected that the converts should speak with new tongues." In the fifth century Chrysostom wrote, "Whosoever was baptized in apostolic days, he straightway spoke with tongues...and this made manifest to them that were without that it was the Spirit in the person speaking." During the fifteenth century there were great revivals in southern Europe with the manifestations of "new tongues." This miraculous manifestation was common among the

Waldenses and Albigenses. (*ibid.*).

The *Encyclopedia Britannica* has recorded the following, "...glossolalia occurred among the mendicant friars of the 13th century, the little prophets of Cevennes, the Camisards, the Jansenists, and the Irvingites. Tradition has it that the gift of tongues was found also among the early Quakers and Shakers, as well as among the converts of John Wesley and George Whitefield; and St. Francis Xavier and St. Vincent Ferrer are said to have possessed it. In modern times glossolalia has been found chiefly among Holiness and Pentecostal groups..." (*Encyclopedia Britannica*, 1972 ed., vol.22: p.75).

> TONGUES, GIFT OF (Glossolalia; Gr. Glossa, "tongue," lalia, "talking"). coherent incoherent utterances of deeply religious individuals, who feel especially blessed and "gifted." The speaker's statement is presumed to contain a message despite the unintelligibility of many of the words. Only infrequently do these "words" have any meaning in themselves, hence it often becomes necessary to have the message translated into the vernacular of the audience either by the speaker or by persons believed to possess a similar gift, "the interpretation of tongues."
>
> Tongue speaking manifested itself early in the Christian experience. At Pentecost (Acts 2) the gift appeared as a sign of the indwelling of the Holy Spirit which marked the character of the earliest Christians. On this occasion it probably was an unpremeditated, unprecedented manifestation of "genuine" glossolalia, incoherent except for ejaculatory words and phrases recognized by the crowds. The apostle Paul referred to it as a spiritual gift (*charisma*; 1Cor.12-14) and claimed that he possessed exceptional ability in that gift (1Cor.14:18). The account in Acts (4:31; 8:14-17; 10:44-48; 11:15-17; 19:1-7) indicates that in the beginning of the Christian Church the phenomenon reappeared wherever conversion and commitment to Christianity occurred. In times the church began to expect and very nearly demand its manifestation to verify the possession of the Holy Spirit; the gift was well on its way toward becoming a sacrament. Thus Paul (1Cor. 14:26) shows that tonguespeaking early entered the Christian service of worship at times other than

conversion and baptism. The longer ending of Mark (16:17) also has a later reference to the phenomenon. (*ibid. Encyclopedia Britannica*).

Tertullian, the outstanding third-century theologian "...was concerned primarily with 'the operation of the power to speak in strange tongues.'" (*The Phenomenon of Pentecost*, p.52). He apparently spoke in tongues himself, since the encyclopedic references declare that he was noted for his "rigorous defense" of tongues and prophecy. It would hardly seem feasible that one of such stature would place himself in guardianship of a gift of which he was not partaker. The non-participants are the ones who fight hardest against the Holy Ghost. "Tertullian held the overriding sin of the Catholics to be that they quarrel with the Paraclete [Holy Ghost] deny the New Prophecy and refuse to receive the Spirit." (*Tertullian: A Historical and Literary Study*, p.43).

TAKING ON THE BRIDEGROOM'S NAME

Tertullian was not only concerned with the language of the Bride but also with the name that she would receive in her espousal; the name of the Bridegroom.

"Wherever the Rule of Faith, which was rooted in the formula of the baptismal commission, formed the fundamental basis of Christian belief, and wherever the data supplied by this Rule of Faith were interpreted in the forms of the Logos speculation, there was constantly in progress a strenuous effort to attain clarity as to the relations of the distinctions in the Name designated by the terms Father, Son, and Holy Ghost" (*Studies In Tertullian and Augustine*, p.103).

The Bride gives herself through repentance and water baptism. She receives her husband in Spirit baptism. One without the other is incomplete. The two combined are the "one baptism" of Ephesians 4:5.

The union between the Bride and Bridegroom is more intimate than any other. The inner room is the place of mutual giving and receiving: the sharing of love. The heavenly language of the Bride is a means of gaining entrance to this room, like a mantra. Once you have learned to enter the room, allow yourself to be led of the Spirit as to the mode of the prayer, silence or outward expression. Sometimes we need to just sit still and absorb. The relationship would lose harmony without the close intimacy that comes by sharing. The expression would become empty. A person would soon find that he was no longer in the inner room but rather in the outer court. We need a balance. Yesu said, "I am the portal: by me if any man enter in, he shall be saved, and he shall go in and out" (John 10:9).

SPIRIT AND THE WORD

It is important to remember Yesu's words, "God is a Spirit and those who worship him must worship in Spirit and in truth." He also said, "Thy word is truth" (John 4:24; 17:17). Those who have the word but not the Spirit are dead. The Spirit is life. Also, to worship in the euphoria of the Spirit without the truth of the Word is perilous. God often speaks to us through the Bible and confirms it by his Spirit. Other times he speaks to us in the spirit and confirms it in his word.

As you become proficient in the inner room experience your life actually becomes a prayer. You can walk in the Spirit without leaving the presence of God.

Every prophet of God, who ever existed has been to the inner room. When you achieve the mystical marriage, you can learn to spend every waking, walking, working moment in the inner room. As you carry out your daily activities, you will be constantly aware of the presence of God, that he is in you and you are in him, embracing one another within the inner room.

God is omnipresent, everywhere, in everything and everyone. He is in all of his creation. He is in every human being, in every cell, in every atom. We just need to learn to make the mental and spiritual connections and then we can know the physical connection as well.

CLEANSE THE TEMPLE

When you are filled with the Holy Spirit, God is in you in a special way, you receive his divine nature. If the temple is broken down and cluttered with trash, the glory of Yahweh is not in it. We must keep the temple clean both spiritually and physically.

> During the Hebrew feasts especially, the Court of the Gentiles became a public market place. To the pilgrims from Palestine or abroad, the hawkers installed under the porticoes or in the great open square sold oxen, sheep, and everything else necessary for the temple sacrifices, while the money changers behind their improvised counters were ready to exchange the various types of Palestinian coinage for the foreign money of the faithful returned from elsewhere. Only after passing through this inferno of stench and noise did one reach the place of expiation, where only the Israelite might enter and cleanse himself of his sins before God, in silence and in prayer. (*The Life of Christ*, p.46).

If we are not already flesh-and-blood Israelites, we become spiritual Israelites when we are born again of the water and the Spirit. We have gained access to the inner room of the temple but sometimes we have to wade through garbage to get there. "The high priest was the chief minister of public worship and head of all the services in the Temple." (*ibid.* p.48). Yesu is our great High Priest. Let him come in and cleanse your temple of all its filth. Let him cast out the money changers.

BE A SAINT NOT A SINNER

Our own negative thoughts can also influence evil upon us. Proverbs 23:7, tells us that as a man "thinketh in his heart, so is he." Once you have repented of your sins (*i.e.* turned away from your mistakes) and have been baptized for remission of sins, stop trying to convince yourself that you are still a sinner. The Scriptures never refer to the Spirit-filled believer as a sinner. He/she is a saint, one set apart in the church (Greek, *ekklesia*, the "called out" ones) of God. If you keep telling yourself that you are a sinner, you will be a sinner. If you say, "I have an evil mind," you will have an evil mind. We continually program ourselves with our thoughts and deeds by reinforcing our cellular memories.

Rather, say, "I have the mind of Christ. I will not think evil. I have received the righteousness of Christ. I am no longer a sinner. I will not yield to the lusts of the flesh. I will not be imprisoned by the bondage of sin. I live in the freedom of the inner room. God is in me and I am in him."

Yesu said, "Let your troubled hearts be at rest, ye believe in God, believe also in me" (John 14:1, *New English Bible*). There is a "peace of God which transcends all understanding" (Philippians 4:7). You can receive the "mind of Christ" (1 Corinthians 2: 16; Philippians 2:5).

"Cast away from you all your transgressions, whereby ye have transgressed; and make you a new heart and a new spirit: for why will ye die..." (Ezekiel 18:31)

THE CODE OF THE HEART CAN BE CHANGED

Reformat your heart energy from negative to positive. The mind is not restricted to the cranium but exists in every cell of your body. The heart is the center of the mind, where all the information of who we are is stored and encoded.

The mind or memory in our cells can be changed. Habits and addictions can be deleted from your cellular memory.

Thoughts that we dwell upon are reinforced and become embedded deeply into the cellular memory. Things we do routinely get securely embedded.

Our personality traits are all encoded into our cells. By changing our routines, thoughts, and actions, we are changing our heart. We can actually reprogram our cellular memories, and thus orchestrate our own destinies.

This is your life. Take charge of it. Make your heart a positive force, for a good life here on earth and for a link to the source beyond the veil.

"Let this mind be in you that was in the anointed Yesu."

"The wages of sin is death; but the gift of God is eternal life, through Yesu Christ our Yahweh." (Romans 6:23).

In the New Testament the word that is translated "sin" means to miss the mark, simply a mistake. The word translated "repent" means to change, or turn around. In modern English terms, it is simply stating, "turn away from your mistakes, change." This reaffirms Ezekiel 18, where we are told if a righteous man becomes evil, all of his righteousness will be forgotten and he will inherit death; but if a sinner turns from his mistakes (he changes) all of his wrong will be forgotten. He will be considered righteous and will inherit life.

Yahweh said that he would live inside of his people. He came to earth as Yesu, suffered, died, was entombed and resurrected, after which he ascended to heaven and began the outpouring of his Spirit in fulfillment of his promised covenant:

"For this is the covenant that I will make with the house of Israel after those days, saith Yahweh; I will put my laws into their mind, and write them in their hearts: and I will be to them a God, and they shall be to me a people: And they shall not teach every man his neighbor, and every man his brother, saying, Know Yahweh: for all shall know me, from the least to the greatest. For I will be merciful to their unrighteousness, and their sins and their iniquities will I remember no more." (Hebrews 8:10-12).

Changing your heart and mind will reprogram your cells and eliminate the negative factors as though they were never there at all. In essence you become a new creature ready for the final call.

Blessings and Glory to all who bring their Ego into submission. Curses to those who do not.

> Tonight when you rest, do not allow the senses to suggest weakness or weariness; instead, allow your spiritual atmosphere within and without to enfold and invigorate you, until you are conscious of spiritual conquest before you sleep. Your whole body will be renewed by this holy baptism, and your awakening in the morning will be a triumph and a joy. The effect of this is a sweet cleansing of mind and body. So much is done during the hours of sleep and darkness. We pray that you may truly say: "Awake or asleep, I am still with thee." [Ps. 139:18] Cease from worry. (*Christ in You*, p.21).

Are you in the inner room, or imprisoned in the satanic dungeons of Babel? The Pagans gathered to worship in elaborately adorned temples, but God does not dwell in temples made by man (Acts 7:48; 17:24). As opposed to house meetings, the early Catholics utilized the pagan temples for their own worship and rituals. Yahweh says, "Come out." The early Christians were called out; God is still "calling out a people for his name" (Acts 15:14).

You should be dwelling in the "secret place of the most High," the inner room, the portal of heaven that reaches from inside of you to beyond the confines of the universe all the way into eternity.

~FIN~

BACK-WORD

THE END FROM THE BEGINNING

You have the ability to transport from the center of your mind directly to the Holy of Holies in heaven.

If you are willing to change and to dedicate some effort and time, the proper forms of meditation will carry you to wonderful places heretofore unknown by you.

Yahweh knows the end from the beginning (Isaiah 46:10). He always knew the exact moment you would make contact with him. And he has waited for the appointed time.

Set your heart to be disciplined and trained in a new direction of personal communication with the Divine. Start with a repentant heart desiring to meet God, and learn to practice the perfect form of meditation. If you do not yet believe in Christ, don't let that stop you. Try it anyway; come as you are and you may find Christ in the process.

In fact when you find God you do find Christ because they are inseparable, these two are one in spirit.

No one comes to the father except through Christ (John 14:6) and no one comes to Christ unless the father draws him (John 6:44). When you have the Holy Spirit you have the father and the son. The Holy Spirit and the spirit of God and the spirit of Christ are One (see Romans 8:9-14). When asked what is the great command, Christ quoted the Shema from Deuteronomy 6:4-9, "Hear O Israel, Yahweh is our God, Yahweh is One: You shall love Yahweh your God with all your heart, soul, and might."

EPILOGUE

SEVENTY-FOUR WITNESSES

The most sacred verse to the Israelite people is the Shema, "Hear o Israel Yahweh is our God, Yahweh is One" (Deuteronomy 6:4;

although Jews do not pronounce Yahweh). In the Hebrew Torah when certain letters are printed larger than normally, as we find in this verse, it has been done this way to draw our attention so we might search out their meaning. In the Shema passage the first and last words catch our attention for this reason. The last letter of the first word is an overly large *Ayin* (ע) and the last letter of the last word is a very large *Daleth* (ד). The letters *Ayin-Daleth*, עד, spell a word meaning "witness." *Ayin-Daleth*, עד, is also the way to write the number 74. This witness gives special significance to the number seventy-four. Write these letters in reverse, דע, and it says "knowledge." So knowledge and witness are inseparable and combine to reveal truth. *Ayin* is a portal and *Daleth* is a door.

In Exodus 24:9-11, seventy-four witnesses saw Yahweh God above a "transparent work of sapphire like the body of heaven in his brightness." Similarly, Ezekiel saw the sapphire throne and God above it (Ezekiel 1:26 & 10:1).

"Like the body of heaven in his brightness." What is the "body" of heaven? Were they actually seeing the energy pattern of the image of God in which man was created? The energy pattern of the tree of life, with its *sephirot*, sapphire spheres?

We are learning, or have learned, to meditate and connect to the presence of God. In Hebrew the word *lamad* (למד) means "To learn." It has the numerical value of 74. The word for "Meditation," *higaion*, (הגיון) also equals 74. We have seen the wonderful significance of this number 74, and we are "Witnesses" (עד=74).

LAST WORD

FEELING UNWORTHY

You feel that you cannot make yourself holy enough to approach God. You are right. None of us can. That is why you must come as you are. The only prerequisite is a repentant heart, i.e. a heart willing and wanting to change. The rest is through his grace. When you make the connection the change will naturally follow. The wonderful presence of God is a transforming agent. His pure love will show you the way. Not that God will make you something you do not want to be, rather the love you feel will give you the desire to willingly change on your own, and the grace he bestows upon you will give you the power and conviction to make those changes happen.

When you begin to have success in your meditation and find yourself in that special place where God dwells, you will be at the point of realization when you simply know. All doubt will be gone. All loneliness will be gone. All fear of death will be gone. A newness of life will be felt in a universe that is both infinitely small and infinitely large, simultaneously. And you are one with it. You are a microscopic speck in the vast cosmos yet it is all inside of you, like the tiniest seed, and within that seed is the ever expanding universe, seemingly without end.

You already have everything. You just do not know it.

God is always with you, good or bad, right or wrong. If you feel cut off it is not that he has left you but that your sins and iniquities have separated you (Isaiah 59:1-2). If you are still alive then God is still in you. There is still hope. You need only to repent, change your mind and turn away from your mistakes. If we change he is just and faithful to forgive us (1 John 1:9).

If you feel a million miles away from God and think there is no hope for you that is just a trick of the adversary to plant despair in your heart. He knows that according to Scripture, what you believe in your heart will be done unto you. So if he can make you believe that you are lost, then you are lost. Don't bite that bait. Believe God, that he has no pleasure in the death of the wicked but that he turn from his evil ways and live, and believe that Christ came not to condemn but to save the lost. Believe that you will be forgiven in accordance to the Scriptures. You have all the hope in the world waiting for you in the inner room, the holy of holies within you. Try your faith and enter now.

~TIME TO BEGIN~

NOTES:

Other Apocalyptic writings:
http://www.nkox.homestead.com/writings.html

See Norbert Kox artwork:
http://www.apocalypsehouse.com

NOTES:

NOTES:

www.ingramcontent.com/pod-product-compliance
Lightning Source LLC
Chambersburg PA
CBHW051708040426
42446CB00008B/771